THE LE

God's timing is perfect

THE
LEE ABBEY
STORY

RICHARD MORE

eagle

Eagle
Guildford, Surrey

British Library Cataloguing in Publication Data. A catalogue
record for this book is available from the British Library.

Published by Eagle, an imprint of Inter Publishing Service
(IPS) Ltd, St Nicholas House, 14 The Mount, Guildford, Surrey
GU2 5HN.

ISBN No: 0 86347 143 9

Typeset by Light Technology Ltd., Fife, Scotland
Printed by HarperCollins, Glasgow

Contents

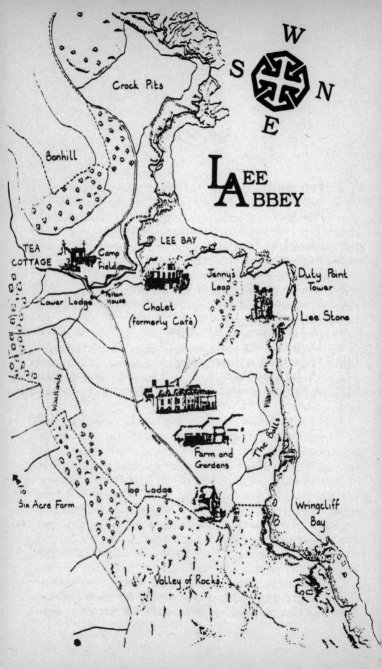

Foreword

When, in the Diocese of Coventry some years ago we were launching a new 'Call to Mission' in our Cathedral at Christmas-time, there was a rather striking act of worship. The large carved figures from the Cathedral crib, of the wise men, the shepherds, the animals and Joseph and Mary, were carried out one by one and each set in place with a prayer said by the whole congregation. Finally the baby was brought and placed in the crib. Only then did the whole grouping find its real meaning.

This movement seemed to suggest not only that this is where the whole creation falls into place, but also that to spread that message, to evangelise, is *to create the context within which Christ can be found*. You could describe it as the context in which *He* can come to find us.

And that context surely has to be corporate. It is through the struggle to find the right pattern of relationships to the creation and to each other that human beings eventually begin to arrive at the truth.

This was the principle that Roger de Pemberton and the founders of Lee Abbey hit upon. They found that in a holiday gathering, in which people have come together in relaxation and friendship, right patterns can be grasped quite spontaneously, naturally and freely by the presence and person of Christ, through the Spirit at work amongst them.

The beautiful house by the sea, which they eventually bought and made into a setting for such encounters, became a place where countless seekers were

to make this discovery. They could all echo Gerard
Manley Hopkins's words in his poem, 'In the Valley
of the Elwy':

> I remember a house where all were good
> To me, God knows, deserving no such thing:
> Comforting smell breathed at very entering,
> Fetched fresh, as I suppose, off some sweet
> wood . . .

There is a hint here of the sweet wood not only of the
hearth, but also of the Cross.

Lee Abbey, through all its varied phases and the
successive styles and strands of its witness over the
years, has sought to constitute a household of faith
where this kind of homecoming can be provided for
many. The secret has always been the way of the
Cross. It is only through the constant corporate rhythm
of repentance and forgiveness and of the release of gifts
in the shared life of the communities that guests can
ever be brought to that central reality. This book gives
a clear and perceptive account of the whole inspiring
history.

But there is a crucial question, which is posed not
only for the Lee Abbey movement, but for our whole
Church by this vivid story. The central quest for the
creating of a home where, in Christ, the fragmented
and homeless spirits of people in our time can find healing and our society reach out towards wholeness, has to
prove strong enough to prevail in a broken world.

Teams going out from these communities are striving
to work out the same pattern of witness in local
churches. The London Lee Abbey Community has
sought to develop the same theme amongst international students. And the little Lee Abbey Communities
in a housing estate or an inner city area are making
perhaps the most vital attempt of all to embody the

message amongst the most outwardly disadvantaged people of our society.

But this excellent story makes clear that when Lee Abbey, Devon, has offered opportunities to look at a Christian response to social issues, rather than solely say, at prayer or healing, there have been fewer takers. And when the new 'Lee Abbey Three' small urban households have sought to recruit members, it has been difficult to find many people willing to come forward.

Perhaps this is going to be the supreme test of this remarkable movement. Can the Lee Abbey houses enable both the members of their communities *and* those who through them come to find Christ, to make a place where, as in the original stable, amongst the poor and vulnerable of our society Christ can be found.

> A place where God was homeless,
> And all shall be at home ...

Lee Abbey still has so much to give our Church and our world that it is my prayer that those who read this book responsively may come forward to help us to answer this last question.

Simon Barrington-Ward
Bishop of Coventry
Chair: Lee Abbey Council

The Bishop's House
Coventry
May 1995

Introduction

It was almost fifteen years ago, while I was a member of the Lee Abbey Community in Devon, that I wrote a book to record something of the remarkable work of God in the founding and development of the ministry of Lee Abbey. That book *Growing in Faith* was published by Hodder & Stoughton in 1982, but has been unavailable for many years.

Now with the Golden Jubilee in September 1995 of the purchase of the house on the North Devon coast, I have largely revised and updated that book.

I am most grateful to both past and present members of the Lee Abbey Communities who have helped me to sense what God has been doing through Lee Abbey over these last few years. I would record my special thanks to David Wavre of Eagle for all his help; to Audrey Martin-Doyle for the material on Lee Abbey in Aston in Chapter 13; to Jenny Hellyer and David Talbot for many helpful comments on the manuscript; to Gill Muller formerly of the Lee Abbey Community in Devon for the map of the Lee Abbey Estate, and especially to my secretary at St James' Porchester in Nottingham, Rosemary Wilson, who has worked many extra hours to type the manuscript. As I wrote in the introduction to *Growing in Faith*, I hope that the facts that I have recorded are accurate; the opinions and reflections are purely my own. With Jack Winslow, who wrote the first book about Lee Abbey back in 1955 I would again write 'we could easily give the appearance of presumption, and of a desire to glorify Lee Abbey rather than to advance the Kingdom of God.

If at any point we are near to doing this we would ask the reader to forgive us ...' I continue to make the same request.

St James' Porchester, Nottingham.
Easter 1995

Prologue

The famous Valley of Rocks, situated on the very edge of Exmoor near the village of Lynton, presents a spectacular sight. On the one side is the steep hillside littered with small boulders and covered with gorse and bracken, while on the other rise great mounds of rock which drop away into the sea, thus creating in one place one of the highest sea cliffs in England. The weird shapes created by the rocks and the bleakness of the landscape have caused it to be compared to the surface of the moon. Even today it is not hard to imagine the legendary John Ridd riding through this valley to consult Mother Meldrum about his beloved Lorna Doone.

Among the visitors to the Valley of Rocks one afternoon in June 1932 was a young curate from Cheltenham, spending a few days holidaying with his sister. It was their first visit, and after looking at the Valley of Rocks itself, they decided to follow the road to see where it led. As they walked uphill, it looked as if the road was coming to a dead end, but suddenly rounding a bend they could see that they were walking down through another wider and very different valley. There were fields on either side; the hillside was wooded; and there was a small golf course. Passing an imposing, ivy-clad stone tower, they continued down the road and a most magnificent view came into sight. The valley, bordered by steep woodlands on either side, sloped down to a small sunlit bay. Beyond that could be seen another bay, and beyond that yet another series of cliffs rising majestically out of the sea. As the previous valley had been austere and barren, so this one was welcoming and lush. The scene was breathtaking in its beauty.

Turning to look at the building which enjoyed this exquisite view, they saw a large Victorian mansion, much of its exterior hidden by creepers, nestling in the slope of the hillside. Wondering what such a magnificent building could be, they retraced their steps back to the tower, to find that a notice-board provided the answer.

THE LEE ABBEY HOTEL
*An Historic House remodelled
and brought up to date*

They looked wistfully at the tariff. 'One thing is certain, you and I will never stay there,' said the young man. And they continued their walk down to the bay.

Chapter 1
Towards the Conversion of England

At the time of his holiday in 1932, Roger de Pemberton was a curate in Cheltenham. It was to be another ten years before he visited Lee Abbey again, but God was already laying the foundation for the part that he was to play with others in establishing a ministry based on that remote West-Country hotel.

Roger was a Christian with a strong evangelical background, and a deep desire to bring people to personal faith in Jesus Christ. Like many of his contemporaries, he had become involved in leading campaigns run by The Children's Special Service Mission (CSSM) in the late 1920s. During his time at Cambridge, first as an undergraduate at St Catherine's College and then as an ordinand at Ridley Hall, three successive Easters found him running a mission at Cheltenham directed mainly at the Boys' and Ladies' Colleges. However, 1929 saw the last of these campaigns as the leaders felt that they were getting into a rut. Yet with over a hundred contacts they were reluctant to allow these to lapse, so they were looking for some way of following them up with regular Christian teaching.

It was then that the idea of a magazine was mooted, and although Roger had had no experience of publishing, he had no shortage of enthusiasm. Unable to get financial backing from CSSM he decided to produce the magazine himself. This was the same determination that was later to be needed when the time came for founding Lee Abbey. Before the first copy was produced in 1930, around 3,000 subscribers had been procured. The magazine was called *The Pathfinder*, and proved very popular, doubling its circulation in three years. Soon the whole project had to be put on a more organised business footing than had been possible at the beginning, when it was edited in his bedroom at his parents' home in Worthing. Now full-time staff were needed to edit and distribute it.

The magazine was different from others of those days in that it sought to present a mixture of items. Each issue would contain a number of general, secular articles of interest to young people set alongside those with a direct spiritual challenge.

In 1935, with the magazine well-established, Roger sought some way of building on the clear response to *The Pathfinder* and of bringing its readers together. He hit on the idea of running a summer holiday houseparty. He consulted a handbook of private schools and found suitable premises for the month of August at Oldfield School in Swanage in Dorset. Renting the school from August 3rd to the 31st, he persuaded a number of friends to come and help as leaders, including J B Phillips, later to become well-known as an author and biblical translator. The holiday was advertised in *The Pathfinder*, offering 'a holiday houseparty for single people under twenty-five'.

This attracted groups from all walks of life. The programme deliberately was not fully organised, but contained all the elements expected of that sort of a holiday – outings, picnics and boat trips, concluding with a grand concert. One day there was even an air display from Sir Alan Cobham. The houseparty proved to have a great spiritual impact; not that anyone was forced to attend meetings or the evening epilogues – indeed nothing was regarded as compulsory – but the atmosphere generated by a large group of Christians together on holiday proved very powerful. Some who were nominal Christians discovered the living Christ for the first time, others rediscovered a purpose for their Christian lives. Away from their homes and their work, many of the young people felt free to talk openly about their hopes, needs and fears.

The houseparty had been a great success and was clearly something to be repeated. Two houseparty centres were taken for the summer of the next year and three for the summer of 1937. The running of *The Pathfinder* had become a full-time job and in 1936 Roger left his parochial work to concentrate on it. This also enabled him to hire centres and run houseparties at other times of the year. By now Roger was convinced of the powerful means of evangelism provided by holiday houseparties. A new idea began to formulate in his mind: why not have a permanent centre available throughout the year for this work? A few possibilities were explored, but for the moment nothing materialised.

By 1939 the total number attending summer houseparties had risen to over 800 and the programme of holiday activities with an epilogue each evening was well-established. However, as the war became more and more inevitable, the houseparties of that year were not completed. After only six days, a party at Château d'Oex in Switzerland were advised to return home, and caught the last regular express to Paris.

At Bodelwyddan Castle in North Wales members of the houseparty began to get telegrams recalling them to work, and by the middle of the second week the houseparty was badly depleted. On the Thursday everybody went home. The secretary of that houseparty, responsible for arranging the special train to get people away, was an ordinand named Gordon Strutt who was to play a very significant part in the next stage in the founding of Lee Abbey.

The outbreak of the war halted the work of *The Pathfinder*. A paper shortage meant that the magazine could not be produced and there seemed to be no place for holiday houseparties in a country at war. Roger had returned to full-time parochial work, but God was preparing other men with a similar vision. Gordon Strutt was to bring together the two men who would be at the centre of the establishment of Lee Abbey.

By 1942 Gordon was ordained and a curate at St Paul's Carlton-in-the-Willows in Nottingham. One day a parishioner asked him to meet her Uncle Leslie who was staying with her family.

Now in his mid-forties, Leslie Sutton had been through a very difficult period in his life. Yet that day it was his deep faith in the living Christ that was most apparent. Leslie shared with Gordon his vision for the Church of England and what he believed God was going to do. Slowly the story of his life began to emerge, as he spoke with the stammer which had been with him since childhood. At the age of thirteen he had committed his life to Christ through the ministry of the children's evangelist, Hudson Pope. During the First World War he had been seriously wounded in the landing at Gallipoli. He was invalided out, as 'an incurable deaf mute', yet through the prayers of his family, after eighteen months of silence, he regained his speech. Convinced that God had spared his life for a purpose, he felt called to the mission field and went out to the Belgian Congo with what was to become WEC – The Worldwide Evangelisation Crusade. After only two years, however, Leslie's health forced him to return to England, where he became adjutant for WEC at their Missionary Training Colony in Upper Norwood.

Whilst at Norwood he became engaged to another member of the WEC community, Elisabeth Hand. They were both members of the Church of England and longed to see what they experienced at WEC becoming part of the life of the Anglican Church, but they could find little sympathy for their Anglican loyalties among their WEC colleagues. So, after much prayer, they decided to leave WEC after their marriage, with the specific purpose of starting some work that would seek to bring revival within the Church of England. While dressing for her wedding, Elisabeth noticed for the first time a suspicious lump on her breast. A week later the doctor diagnosed widespread, inoperable cancer. She had to go to hospital straight away for daily treatment, but after only eight months of marriage she died.

Thus it was a man broken, but undefeated, who talked to Gordon Strutt. As he spoke, Gordon remembered a letter he had recently received from Roger de Pemberton, who was now vicar of St Nicholas' Church in Rochester. The letter had asked if Gordon could suggest anyone who could come and join Roger on the staff at St Nicholas' to work especially amongst men: Gordon sensed that here might be just the man. Leslie Sutton set off to Rochester to visit Roger for the weekend and did not return!

Since Roger de Pemberton had become vicar of St Nicholas' there had been no shortage of activity in the parish, and there was plenty to keep Leslie occupied. The congregation was growing quickly, attracted by the charismatic personality of the vicar and the strong, direct preaching. Roger was a man full of new ideas, but he did not allow his literary skills to lie dormant. Much of what he had learned in producing *The Pathfinder* was applied to the parish magazine, *The Rochester Review*, and its publication was eagerly awaited by many people who had little contact with St Nicholas'. As well as the normal parish news, he included many articles similar to those which had made *The Pathfinder* so popular.

As the war stretched on into its third year, Roger's thoughts again began to turn to houseparties, and he wondered whether he could recommence the very successful work that had been halted in 1939. He wrote to the Ministry of Labour to try out the idea and received a warm response from their Welfare Officers. In August 1942 he rented a school in St Austell, Cornwall and the houseparties were restarted.

It was clear there was a real need for such holiday houseparties during wartime and it was decided to run two more in August of the next year. St Austell was booked again and the Welfare Officers of the Ministry of Labour undertook much of the recruitment. To find another centre, Roger returned to Truman and Knightly's *Guide to Public Schools* which had proved so helpful in finding suitable premises in the past. A supplement in the back of the war-time edition included a list of addresses of all the schools which had been evacuated. It was here that Roger again came across the name of Lee Abbey, Lynton and memories of that June afternoon, ten years earlier, came flooding back. A letter from the headmaster indicated that the building might be available for use in August and so, together with Leslie, he went down to inspect the premises.

The intervening ten years had not been kind to Lee Abbey and its estate; it was a very different sight that confronted Roger and Leslie as they inspected the building in the pouring rain.

The main building had been erected by the local squire, Charles Bailey, who had purchased the property in 1841. In keeping with the fashion of that period he had adopted a Neo-Gothic design for the house, including two stone follies in the form of ruined towers. Even the name was adapted to the spirit of the age and the Lee Manor of Lorna Doone became the more stately Lee Abbey.

In due course the estate passed to his son, on whose death in 1921 it was divided up and the house with 360 acres was purchased by a hotel company. With great enthusiasm they enlarged the accommodation by building a new bedroom wing, and laid out the golf course, but this was not an easy time for such a smart hotel, set in a relatively remote part of the country. The economic situation soon meant that little money could be spent on the fabric of the building, and the declaration of war set the seal on its fate: it went bankrupt. The official receivers, into whose hands Lee Abbey then passed, had little difficulty in finding a use for the building. It was the start of the blitz and many boarding schools in the South-East, their own buildings commandeered by the Army, were looking for accommodation to which they could evacuate their pupils. The West Country was an obvious area and there was some competition to acquire suitable premises. So it was at the time of Dunkirk, in June 1940, that Brambletye Preparatory School from East Grinstead in Sussex moved their pupils, furniture, equipment and all that remained of their teaching and domestic staff to take up residence in Lee Abbey.

It was now a very dilapidated house that Roger and Leslie visited. The building which had looked so impressive in 1932 was completely daubed with camouflage, lest any German bombers returning down the Bristol Channel from raids over Bristol, might choose to jettison their remaining bombs on a prominent building. The octagonal room, built as a music room by Charles Bailey and subsequently used as the hushed lounge of the smart hotel, was now the noisy dining room for 100 small boys. The fine bedrooms, their carpets gone, were dormitories; the golf course had disappeared under grass and weeds; and the café on the beach had fallen victim to vandals. Yet they were not deterred. An arrangement was made with the headmaster to rent the house for the following August and for the first time a holiday houseparty was advertised for Lee Abbey at the cost of £2.10s per week.

As today, Lee Abbey proved to be an ideal setting for a holiday. There were plenty of opportunities for walks on the numerous paths within the estate, on the coastal path to Hunter's Inn with its magnificent view, or further afield up on to Exmoor; Lee Bay provided a safe beach from which to swim; there was a tennis court; for those who just wanted to be lazy, there was a lawn at the front of the house from which to take in the magnificent view, and above all it was peaceful.

But the living conditions were primitive even by wartime standards. The only furniture in the house belonged to the school, so most people slept in dormitories with two or three others, on beds which were designed for young boys! Many came down in the morning complaining of aching limbs and lumps in the mattresses! The locks on the bathroom doors had long since disappeared, and there was quite a lot of truth in the rumours that rats had been seen around the store-sheds in the inner courtyard and that there were cockroaches in the kitchen. All the guests were expected to share in domestic duties, washing up, laying tables, preparing vegetables and serving meals, and this was all considered to be part of the fun of the holiday.

As with his other houseparties, this first holiday at Lee Abbey was run by a team of committed Christians invited by Roger from among his many contacts. They came as guests, but arranged the programme and were responsible for the pastoral care of all the visitors. Each day concluded with the epilogue, not the brief talk with which that word is often associated today, but a full-length session in which the claims of Christ were clearly presented. This proved again to be a holiday in which many people took a decisive step in their Christian lives. A letter from *The Rochester Review* in 1944 gives an impression of the impact that Lee Abbey holidays were making.

It was the first real break that I had had for five years and there was God right in the middle of the team, reaching out and touching each one of us, either directly or indirectly. My own experience was one of drawing closer to God and the marvel of His prevailing love. One day while we walked to Watersmeet, at one point the water dropped suddenly over a smoothly-flattened rock, about three or four feet – the rocks behind at the side were rough and scratchy – and the thought passed through my mind: 'If only we would let God's love flow over us so the rough patches would be smoothed out and His love would flow out to the other lives that we meet daily.'

It was decided to use Lee Abbey again for houseparties the following August, but already Roger was getting another idea.

When Leslie Sutton joined Roger de Pemberton at Rochester, he brought with him a deep yearning in his heart to see revival come to the Church of England. He knew that prayer changed things and he believed that revival would only come as people prayed. This was his constant theme and he practised what he preached. For almost two years Leslie and Roger with a few others prayed for the revival of the Church.

Their deep concern was being felt in many other quarters. The war had revealed the spiritual poverty of the Church of England. The great movement of population caused by conscription and evacuation revealed just how formal and hollow much British religion had become. For the first time a religious Public Opinion Poll had been taken, organised by Mass Observation. Its conclusions were published under the title 'Puzzled People'; it revealed that the majority of the nation had no Christian belief and that even many church people did not accept some of the fundamentals of the Christian faith – that Jesus was the Son of God or that He had risen from the dead. It was already clear that a massive task was going to face the Church if it were to regain contact with the general population.

It is often said that the Church of England's answer to any problem is to appoint a committee! On this occasion William Temple, the Archbishop of Canterbury, was fully aware of the seriousness and challenge of the situation. As early as 1943 he called together a Commission to 'survey the whole problem of modern evangelism', so that the Church might have a clear strategy when the war was over. It was a diverse group of fifty men and women including Roger de Pemberton and encompassing a wide spectrum of theological opinion who met together for the first time in February 1944, in the Jerusalem Chamber of Westminster Abbey. Yet all shared the special concern and interest in evangelism.

The findings of the Commission were not to be published until the end of the war. The report was clear in its conclusions and did not mince words, even in the title itself: *Towards the Conversion of England*. Fifty years later it still makes challenging reading, as it analyses 'a wholesale drift from organised religion'. It concluded that the Church had become irrelevant to the life and thought of the community in general, demonstrated by the widespread decline in churchgoing and the collapse of Christian moral standards.

The message comes over clearly:

The aim of evangelism is conversion. Conversion is the reorientation of life from self to God through Jesus Christ. Conversion may be sudden ... or conversion may be gradual ... But whether sudden or gradual, it is the birthright of every child of God to be converted ...

We cannot expect to get far with evangelism until three facts are faced. First, the vast majority of English people need to be converted to Christianity. Secondly, a large number of church people also require to be converted, in the sense

of their possessing that personal knowledge of
Christ which can be ours only by the dedication
of the whole self, whatever the cost. Thirdly,
such personal knowledge of Christ is the only
satisfactory basis for testimony to others . . .

It will thus be realised that the really daunting
feature of modern evangelism is not the masses of
population to be converted, but that most of the
worshipping community are only half-converted.

The report did not merely analyse problems; it contained many practical suggestions. The key to evangelism, it suggested, was the clergy who traditionally
had been trained to be pastors rather than evangelists.
Training in evangelism was desperately needed.

For such a situation the paramount necessity is
that the parish clergy as a body should gain a
new vision, fresh hope and the Baptism of the
Holy Spirit. Any forward move, therefore, in evangelism must begin with the clergy themselves,
and with their coming together to gain a new
liberation into the vision of the Glory of God.

The next urgent need described by the report was for
the mobilisation and training of the laity for evangelism. 'The Apostolate of the Laity' had to be rediscovered, not merely theologically, but practically. Among
many suggestions the idea was put forward of small
groups of laity being trained in a parish to go out as
a mission team to other places.

William Temple had died in 1944, before the report
was published. When it did appear in the following year
it was welcomed by many within the Church who felt
that it reinforced their own conviction that God was
calling for a great revival. However, to the main body
of the Church of England such suggestions were too

revolutionary, and many chose to 'leave it for future debate' and so forget all about it.

Roger's own thinking on evangelism, was totally in step with that of the report. It was during the first houseparty at Lee Abbey in 1943, over a cup of coffee at the Tea Cottage, that Roger talked about his thoughts for the future of Lee Abbey with one of the team. This latest scheme was very simple; he wanted to buy the place as a centre for evangelism. His pre-war experience had convinced him of the value of these holiday houseparties for evangelism and Christian training. The headmaster of the school had indicated to him that as soon as the war ended, the school would be returning to Sussex and the property would be up for sale. Its poor state and the fact that few people would be interested in such a large property meant that it would be cheap. Here was a great opportunity to launch out into something entirely new in the Church of England – a permanent centre for evangelism.

Roger's enthusiasm for the scheme was not immediately shared. Where would the money come from for the down-payment of the mortgage, let alone the purchase price? Did he realise that he was thinking of buying a building that was virtually derelict? Was it really likely that there would be sufficient people willing to come to houseparties throughout the summer months? Who was going to run the place? The hotel had gone bankrupt; he might end up the same way.

However, on his return to Rochester he continued to pursue this goal of purchasing Lee Abbey. The headmaster of the school was keen on the idea and even agreed to buy the property himself and in turn sell it to Roger. This would guarantee a lower price for Roger, since the headmaster was the sitting tenant; it would also release the school from any responsibility for damage to the property during their tenancy.

Roger began to circulate a nine-page document among some of his friends spelling out his proposal to buy Lee Abbey. For five months each year, from May to September, it could be used as a permanent houseparty centre. In the winter months it might become a training college in evangelism – a place where laity and clergy could come for training in Christian work, Bible study, etc. Possible developments for the estate were also mooted – the building of summer chalets; the hire of beach huts; a camping site on one of the golf courses; a car park open to the public; a swimming pool at the top of the beach to use when the tide was out. The property would be held by a trust and registered as a charity. The organisation would also be administered by the Trustees who, in the main, would be those engaged in the work.

A vast amount of work was necessary for the purchase of the property – the securing of loans and the setting up of a charity – and as this was begun, a group of people began to come together, convinced that this apparently foolhardy scheme might indeed have the hand of God upon it. As Roger shared the proposal with his contacts, it seemed to be offering exactly the spearhead for evangelism and training that many were convinced was desperately needed. Together they began to pray to discover whether or not this was the will of God. If it were of God, they knew that it would succeed; if not, it would fail – there were certainly plenty of things that could confound the purchase.

One obvious problem was money. It was not until the basic commitment to purchase had been made that Roger received a letter from a firm of London solicitors. On opening it he learnt that a second cousin of his had died and he had been left £6,000, which he offered as a loan for the mortgage down-payment. God was indeed at work.

August 1944 was the second year of holiday house-parties for war workers at Lee Abbey. Yet few of the guests, as they were swimming or playing tennis, knew that indoors the first meeting was taking place to draw up the legal documents necessary for the purchase of the property. On October 18th, the Pathfinder Trust came into being, with seven men responsible for the oversight of its work – Cuthbert Bardsley (Provost of Southwark); Jack Winslow (Chaplain of Bryanston School); Geoffrey Rogers (Candidates Secretary of CMS); Oswald Garrard (a vicar from Bedford); Derek Wigram (a housemaster from Bryanston School); together with Leslie Sutton as Secretary and Roger himself as chairman, they became the Trustees of the Pathfinder Trust and Council of Management of the Pathfinder Fellowship. Each had been carefully chosen by Roger, for he was anxious, not only that they should fully share his own vision for evangelism and lay training, but also that they should be representative of the different recognised groups within the Church. For instance, Jack Winslow was well-known among anglo-catholics and Derek Wigram had many contacts with conservative evangelicals. A third significant influence in the early days of Lee Abbey was the Oxford Group. Both Jack Winslow and Cuthbert Bardsley had once been closely associated with the group, but becoming increasingly unhappy with certain features of its teaching, they had left it. Then, as now, Lee Abbey aimed to serve the whole Church, rather than being identified with any one particular group.

The first task of the Trustees was to approve the arrangements made by Roger for the purchase of the property and the raising of the necessary money. The total cost was £28,000.

As England entered the final year of the war, the purchase arrangements went steadily ahead. For the first time an Easter houseparty was held, followed by a week of prayer and preparation for evangelism. About sixty people attended and it attracted the wide range of Christian experience that had been hoped for, but tensions were apparent, especially among those who were anxious about the influence of the Oxford

Group. If Lee Abbey were going to be an Oxford Group centre, then many would not be associated with it; this suspicion was to dog Lee Abbey in its first years.

In August, two fortnight-long houseparties were arranged at Lee Abbey and Roger had also taken over All Hallows, Rousdon, a school near Lyme Regis. There was a further fortnight designed especially as a holiday training course in evangelism. With their own building now vacated by the Army, Brambletye Preparatory School was ready to return to Sussex. As the houseparty ended, the removal vans moved in and so, on September 8th, 1945, Lee Abbey finally became the property of the Pathfinder Trust.

Chapter 2
The First Year

What a task confronted Leslie Sutton as the furniture vans moved off down the Valley of Rocks. It had already been agreed that as soon as the school vacated the premises Leslie should move from Rochester and take up permanent residence at Lee Abbey as acting warden. Now, with a few volunteer helpers, mainly staying on from the houseparty, he surveyed the vast empty building. Where should they begin?

It is not easy for the person familiar with Lee Abbey today, with its central heating, double-glazed windows and wall-to-wall carpeting, to imagine the state of the building. The last two years of the school's occupation had done nothing to improve things. There were broken windows to repair and inspection underneath the floorboards revealed that much of the wiring was charred and urgently needed replacing. Rats and mice had taken up occupation and above all the place was filthy. In the back yard piles of rubbish, accumulated by the hotel and school, had to be shifted. All this was made more difficult by the acute shortage of tools and building materials at the end of the war.

The building also needed furnishing. Furniture, cooking utensils and crockery were needed for some 150 people and they had nothing. However, as the needs became known, many gifts came in, including clothing coupons which were spent on curtain material. Leslie and his helpers visited nearly every auction within a seventy-mile radius of Lynton, and Roger and his wife Peggy went to all the sales around Rochester, to find beds, mattresses, and furniture.

A further problem was the water and electricity supplies. The estate was too remote to be connected to the mains, but a number of springs produced a very pure supply of drinking water for the house. They also provided the power to drive a Pelton Wheel, which was housed near the beach and generated the electricity for lighting. The school had encountered enormous problems with this, for if the water was too low, or the springs became clogged with leaves, then the lights would flicker, fade and often go out altogether. It was clearly going to be necessary to augment the supply with the diesel generator installed by the hotel company, which had hardly been used – its discovery was to provide Leslie with one of his favourite illustrations for epilogues:

One morning Bert the gardener took me to a big double door in the 'annexe' regions in the back yard. 'Thur be an engine in thur, zur' he said.

We opened it up, but all we could see was a pile of old junk: bedsteads, mattresses, broken mirrors, torn rolls of carpet, discarded kitchen utensils – all thrown in a great tangled heap.

Bert still insisted 'thur be an engine underneath', and as we pulled out the rubbish it came into view – a Rushton and Hornby diesel engine which should have been providing light and power for all the house.

Then men set to work and cleaned and oiled it till it shone, filled its tank with oil, and when all was done two of them grasped the handles of the starting-lever and struggled to turn the wheel.

The engine gave a few hesitating chuffs and then stopped dead. So we wrote to the maker, and he sent us a beautifully illustrated book.

This showed us in every detail how the engine should work.

We carefully followed all the instructions, and tried again. This time there were just a few more chuffs ... and then silence once again. We knew something was radically wrong. There was nothing more we could do to make the engine work. So once more we wrote to the maker, and this time he sent a man, his own representative, one who had been with the firm from boyhood and knew these engines from A to Z – George, a little bowler-hatted Yorkshireman. He lived with us, and got straight down to work. He soon found that the main crank shaft was out of true, and he put in a new one. When he was satisfied that all was in order, and with all our men standing round watching, he connected the engine to the pressure bottle, pulled over the automatic starting-lever, and lo! the big wheel began to turn, slowly at first, but soon settling down to its right rhythm. And the lights came on in the house. Then George, black to the elbows in oil, folded his arms and stood back regarding it lovingly, and said, "Ow I loves to 'ear 'em 'um!'

As the winter progressed, God began to bring together the people needed to run Lee Abbey in its first season. From the beginning it was seen as imperative that those who came to work at any job should be committed Christians, coming because they believed that they were called by God to share in this new work. Slowly posts were filled. Estate manager, secretary, housekeeper, mechanic, cook/caterer, gardeners. In the early hours of June 1st, 1946, the last load of furniture arrived and later that day the opening houseparty began. Although the house was now furnished and habitable, it was going to take a very long time to repair the building thoroughly and reclaim the estate.

'An opening Conference and Dedication for those actively interested in Evangelism and Lee Abbey' was the title for this first week at Pentecost 1946. It was a great gathering including many of the people who had been drawn into this new vision for evangelism over the previous couple of years. Rain fell steadily for most of the week, but Thursday June 5th, the day set aside for the Dedication, dawned a glorious, sunny day. The service took the form of a procession with the Bishop of Exeter, Dr Charles Curzon, the Archdeacon of Barnstaple, many local clergy, the Trustees and conference guests. Singing hymns, the procession wound its way round the building, outside and in, stopping to dedicate the land, the workshops, the chapel and the octagonal lounge.

Roger, as chairman of the Trustees, outlined the events that had led up to that day: 'It was all prayer and faith, and so, please God, it will continue. We are yet in the dark as to a good deal, and yet in considerable need as to a good deal, but we are convinced that where God guides, God provides, and we have not the slightest hesitation in saying that our needs in personnel, in materials, and in finance, will be provided.'

There were three things he believed that Lee Abbey should do:

First, by trying as well as we can in our small way to stir the Church to a greater concern for evangelism, which many of us believe is its primary concern and responsibility today; secondly, to call men and women into an experience of radical conversion. We believe, quite emphatically, that human nature is diseased; that in some way it needs recreating by turning to God through faith in Christ, which brings about a change in life, and regeneration ... thirdly, we are much concerned with the whole question of Christian leadership. One of the things the Church is suffering from is the lack of creative Christian leadership on the part of the laity.

Cuthbert Bardsley, Provost of Southwark, was next to speak in an address that was to prove prophetic both for the nation and for Lee Abbey, as he analysed the needs of the world.

Firstly, was needed 'the creation of confessed and confessing Christians, men and women whose hearts the Lord has touched, who have working experience of the forgiveness and love of Jesus Christ, who know the authority of the Word "Thus saith the Lord", and who are able intelligently to introduce other people to the saving grace of Christ.' The second need was to have not merely lone-wolf Christians, but teams; 'an atom force of spiritual energy that nothing can resist'.

'The Church congregation is often too large a unit for the Spirit to work through effectively. The congregation needs to have at the heart of it a number of cells of dynamic united love.'

He concluded,

There needs to come into the Church a new fighting spirit. There is too much depression about today – too much lack of faith. We have lost faith because so many others have not gone far enough to find faith. It is my passionate belief that Lee Abbey will recover for thousands their faith in God, and will raise the morale of Church and State to militant, pentecostal Christianity.

Any visitor present at Lee Abbey on that momentous day, watching the procession and listening to the speeches, would have had no doubts about Lee Abbey's close links with the Church of England. The vast majority of people present were Anglicans, the Bishop of Exeter led the service. Lee Abbey had been founded by Anglicans and its stated purpose was to

seek the specific renewal of the Church of England. Yet
the Trustees were extremely anxious from the beginning that Lee Abbey should remain independent of the
Church of England establishment. This still remains
true today. The Warden and chaplains are Anglicans
though within the last few years the possibility of
appointing a non-Anglican chaplain has been accepted.
Lee Abbey seeks to serve the whole Church, though not
from a non-denominational standpoint. Members of the
Community come from a wide span of denominations,
from Roman Catholic to Brethren, and in the same way
it is hoped that all the guests who come to stay will feel
equally welcomed and at home whatever their church
tradition.

Between June and the end of September in that
first season, holiday houseparties were held, and some
600 people visited Lee Abbey. With the International
Houseparty and 'Houseparty for Younger Married
Couples and Children under eight years', a successful
pattern was established which would be repeated in
many succeeding years.

The practice of previous years was adopted with
leadership taken by invited guest speakers, who were
responsible for the epilogues. On each houseparty there
were a number of guests who had attended a previous houseparty and were committed Christians. From
them a small team was selected who would meet
together each day to pray for the guests and share
together any problems.

As the letters came back from guests, there was no
doubt that the Holy Spirit had been doing much during
that first summer. There was the young man who after
his conversion declared 'It's just like being born again,'
with no knowledge that he was using the very words of
Jesus Himself. There was a vicar from the Midlands
who had been sent to find out what Lee Abbey was like;
he discovered that he was not right with God, entered
into a new commitment and went back to bear witness

to his Diocesan committee. At one houseparty no fewer than thirty young people professed conversion.

Throughout this time Leslie Sutton had been acting as Warden, but the intention had always been that there should be a permanent pastoral staff at Lee Abbey to run the houseparties and conferences. A long time was spent at the July meeting of the Council of Management discussing the post of Warden, with the result that Roger was appointed as Warden, Leslie Sutton as sub-warden and the Revd J H (Tommy) Thompson as chaplain. Tommy Thompson had joined Roger the previous year in Rochester as associate vicar. So on October 24th the de Pembertons and Thompsons arrived and Roger took up his new post as the first Warden of Lee Abbey.

It soon became clear that in the establishment of Lee Abbey as a centre of evangelism, God's plan was not concerned merely with the restoration of a large Victorian house; he was also building a community of people. In the winter of 1946–7 those whom God had brought together at Lee Abbey began to work out their relationships, though at that time they knew virtually nothing about community life. Indeed it was almost by accident that they discovered they were a community and had to work out the implications.

For centuries the religious communities had played an important part in the life of the Church of England, and a definite pattern was assumed to be basic for everyone living 'the religious life'. It involved a convent or monastery with a single-sex community normally following the Rule of Life laid down by one of the great saints like Francis or Benedict. Many such communities were refounded as a result of the great Anglo-Catholic Revival in the nineteenth century, and evangelical Christians were often suspicious of the idea of a community because of these Anglo-Catholic overtones. The idea that Lee Abbey, with its mixed group of lay people, could be a religious community was hard to grasp. One church dignitary is reputed to have commented that he didn't approve of 'monks and nuns living together'.

Though the size of the Lee Abbey Community has greatly increased, so that it now comprises about sixty adults, the basic principles of Community membership have not altered since the first year. The Community is made up of men and women covering a wide age range; the majority are single, though there are always a number of families, often with children.

At the beginning there were two distinct groups: the permanent and the temporary Community. The former, like Roger and Leslie, were those called by God from different spheres of work to serve at Lee Abbey for an indefinite period. At this time the Lord was bringing together a team of people, many of whom were to stay for a number of years. However, Community membership at Lee Abbey has never been regarded as a life-long commitment, but as one part, albeit very significant, of any person's life.

The majority of Community members will stay for about one or two years, with others coming for just a few months to help during the busy summer season. Some have stayed much longer. Madeleine Wheen was to be Lady Warden for twenty-eight years; Pat Pilditch was Friends' Secretary for twenty-four years; Ursula Kay was at Lee Abbey for twenty-nine years until her death in 1985, and in 1995 Edna Madgwick has been with the Community for forty-four years and Audrey Copping for twenty-seven years.

As the body of Christ is made up of many different parts, so in the Lee Abbey Community God brings together a group of people from diverse backgrounds. Many have trained for a profession: teachers, nurses, social workers, secretaries and accountants. There have often been those who are preparing for ordination or for service overseas, and a number spend a year in the Community before going to college, or beginning a new course of training. It is fascinating to witness the way that God honours His promises and meets the need of the Community; often a particular skill is not discovered until the person has actually joined!

Few have found life in the Community easy; after that first winter Leslie wrote in the Lee Abbey Review 'team work and living in Community is a testing and strengthening experience. It is costly to our individual pride of self-will because each must work as part of the whole and be open to the criticism and advice of others'. Yet the experience has proved enormously enriching even though at the time it might be painful.

One great example from these early days was 'Pop' Hughes, a retired Wiltshire farmer. He came to Lee Abbey in 1946 when his daughter, Betty, was appointed as Head Cook. They lived together at Lower Lodge and Pop was asked to look after the farm and the gardens. So each day he would drive up the hill in his pony-cart drawn by 'Dolly'. Many found him extremely difficult; he did not seem to fit in at all, and he often used to wave his stick and shout at people. Yet as the years went by the Holy Spirit was mellowing Pop, so that when it was time for him to retire from outdoor work it was found that he had a very real pastoral ministry. He would spend much of his time sitting in the small lounge writing letters, or on one of the seats outside just chatting with anyone who came along. Countless people would testify to the enormous help they had received from Pop in his new God-given role as a grandfatherly counsellor. In 1955 Betty moved on from Lee Abbey but Pop remained until his death in 1960.

Another notable feature of the Community since its beginning is that there has been a constant supply of members from overseas. On the Saturday after he had moved in, Roger set off on a tour of the Continent, which included a visit to the Ecumenical Centre at Bossey in Switzerland and also to Holland and France. As well as encouraging many people to come to the

International Houseparty, he was recruiting for the Community, and in March two young Swiss arrived at Lee Abbey. By the next year there were no fewer than eight overseas Community members – four from Holland, one from Denmark and three from Norway – and they were to be the first of a whole succession who have made valuable contributions to the life of the Community. Indeed, in the early years it would have been almost impossible to staff the house without these overseas members. However, the presence in the Community of different European nationalities brought a great deal of pain. Memories of the war were still very fresh; Dutch and German girls living closely together created very real tensions to which the healing, reconciling power of Christ had to be brought.

Central to the life of any Christian community must be worship together. The Community met together at the beginning of the first winter season in 1946 to work out a pattern of worship which it hoped would be expressive of the life of the whole Community, representing, as it did, a very wide spectrum of tradition. There was the need to combine the formal and informal, whilst leaving room for experimentation and the flexibility to adapt as things worked out. They formulated a structure including Holy Communion, Evensong, Bible meditation, daily intercessions and informal prayer.

In the end a very much simpler pattern was adopted and this has changed little over the years. For thirty-five minutes at the beginning of each day except Sunday, there are Community prayers, which all members of the Community are expected to attend unless they are taking their day off. The format varies from day to day and is determined by the members of the Community who take it in turns to lead the worship. One day each week is set aside as Community Day which begins with a corporate Communion service. Experience has proved that it is essential to have a day when the whole Community can be together. There are plenty of other opportunities for prayer together in smaller groups.

The first winter in the Community underlined the very considerable material sacrifice which God required of those whom He brought to Lee Abbey. Each member received their board and keep together with a personal allowance, which varied according to circumstances, but was sometimes as little as ten shillings a week. However, as the winter progressed with no income from guests, Lee Abbey's financial situation became so serious that many were not even receiving this small amount. At one time logs were chopped up from the many fallen trees in the woods and sold in Lynton in order to bring in some money.

Living conditions were also far from easy. There was very little privacy, and nearly everybody had to share a room with one or two others – also it was generally believed that no Community member had a bed with a spring in it! Added to that 1946–7 proved to be the hardest winter for over fifty years. There was no shortage of wood on the estate for fuel, and they were generating their own electricity, but the long spell of snow meant that many vital jobs could not be done. The house was cut off from the outside world for quite a time, and the only way of getting essential supplies was by taking a sledge one and a quarter miles through the drifts to Lynton. Then there was a further hindrance to work – an outbreak of flu that managed to lay low nearly the whole Community.

The hardships of the first year had been expected, but in many ways 1947 was to be even more difficult. Delayed by the fuel crisis, the brochure was sent out very late. This meant that there were far fewer bookings for houseparties than there had been previously. Also the appalling winter meant that fewer people were going on holiday and this general slump in the holiday trade hit Lee Abbey. It was a very disturbing situation, both because of its financial implications and because it seemed to thwart the whole purpose of the place. Further problems arose when Tommy Thompson, the chaplain, resigned in the middle of the summer necessitating a rearrangement of the winter plans. Despite all the discouragements, however, there was a real sense of excitement because they were involved in the work of God.

Plenty of people outside thought that Lee Abbey could not possibly succeed: that it was a waste of time to try to restore this huge building; it would only be a matter of time before they would go bankrupt and have to give it up. Yet the Community knew differently; they were there because God had called them, and because He had called them He was not going to fail them. Theirs was a pioneering spirit.

Chapter 3
Surrendering to Christ

'It really is extraordinary,' said one English lady to another at an Indian Club. 'He sits on the floor with all these natives eating chapattis and other queer things, all with his fingers; and the amazing thing is that he's an Eton man.' However, the other lady mistook 'Eton' for 'Eaten', held up her hands in horror and exclaimed 'Has he!'. In those days nothing was too bad to be believed of a man who 'went native'.

The man who had so horrified the English ladies was Jack Winslow, who in May 1948, arrived as chaplain of Lee Abbey. With the departure of Tommy Thompson, the Council was anxious to find a man from the Anglo-Catholic tradition, who could maintain the balance of churchmanship and who shared their vision for evangelism. Jack Winslow was the obvious choice. He had been involved with Lee Abbey from the beginning as one of the Trustees, and had been a frequent speaker at houseparties; moreover he would soon be completing his appointment as Chaplain of Bryanston School in Dorset.

He was already sixty-five years old when he joined the Community and few people could have imagined that he was to stay for fifteen years. He brought with him not merely the wisdom of age, but also a vast wealth of experience culled from a remarkable ministry.

His father was Rector of Hanworth in Middlesex, and Jack often wrote of his deep gratitude to God for his childhood spent in that Victorian rectory with his four sisters. He went to school at Eton, where with his fellows he serenaded Queen Victoria at Windsor Castle for her Diamond Jubilee, and later as a member of the Volunteer Corps was to line the route at her funeral service in St George's Chapel. After going to Balliol College, Oxford, he was ordained and then went out to India with the Society for the Propagation of the Gospel. However, he found life as a European missionary in India frustrating, and so on returning to India from his first leave, he gathered together a group of young Indian Christians and together they founded a small community, an ashram, and there Indians and Europeans shared a common life of a simple Indian character, with no distinction of race or class, wearing Indian dress and living on a common fund. Through this ashram many Indians of both high and low caste came to faith in Christ.

In his book *A Testament of Thanksgiving*, Jack Winslow described an experience in September 1932 that he always looked upon as a turning-point in his life. He had been asked to help lead a convention for Christians to be held at Jaffna in Sri Lanka (then called Ceylon). On the long journey from Poona to Ceylon he read a book written by a member of the Oxford Group. It impressed him deeply and made him aware of his own personal pride.

> I came to Jaffna and the convention began. A large crowd, mostly of Tamils, filled the old Dutch church evening by evening. About the fifth day it seemed right to give an opportunity for any who so wished to stake out a definite decision for Christ. I had given the address and suggested a time of silence in which we faced what such a decision might mean. In the silence there came to me a strong urge, which I could only interpret as a divine command, to stand up in the pulpit where I

was and tell the congregation that I myself needed to lead the way in making a deeper surrender of my own life to God, mentioning some of the things which I had seen were holding me up. It was not easy. After all, I was there to instruct others, as the leader of the convention. But nothing less would have brought the needed humbling of pride.

After I had said my bit, I invited all those who were prepared to face the cost of all-out commitment to stay behind after the service. Some hundreds stayed. We decided to do nothing hurriedly or under stress of emotion, but to give a day's thought to all that such commitment involved. The next night a large number solemnly took their stand for Christ, some for the first time, some in a deeper dedication . . .

I myself made a fuller dedication of my life than ever before. It was renewal of the very real commitment which I had made at my ordination, but on the deeper level which twenty-five years' experience made possible. The results were astonishing. I awoke the next morning to a new world. New life had flowed into me. I felt as if I had been reborn . . .

But the most significant thing which was given to me on that day was a new outgoing love for people. It is something I find difficult to describe. I had been till then unduly introspective and full of self-concern. I would not say that this has ever entirely vanished, but I did find from Jaffna onwards a new interest in, and care for, the people I met, which introduced me to a richness of fellowship which I had not known before. This was a wonderful gift to me. It was so obviously none of my doing. It was a sheer miracle.

On returning to England Jack served on the Commission that produced *Towards the Conversion of England*, being asked to give the opening devotional session. In June 1940 the BBC had invited him to broadcast a series of three morning services and in response to what he said he received some 10,000 letters.

In bringing Jack Winslow to Lee Abbey, the Lord was providing a person who was to prove very important both in the growth of the Community, and in ministering to literally thousands of guests.

In 1948 God was drawing together several people who were to work together as a team for the next twelve years. On New Year's Eve, Phyllis Lewis arrived to become Assistant Secretary, and soon also first Secretary of the Friends of Lee Abbey. It was not long before Community members began to notice something about Phyllis – she was clearly in love with Leslie Sutton. Phyllis and Leslie were the first of many couples who have been brought together by God through their membership of the Community. At the end of the houseparty season in September, they were married in Lynton Parish Church with a reception in the octagonal lounge.

Jack Winslow joined the Community in April, and one week later Madeleine Wheen arrived. It was in 1945 that a friend had persuaded her to organise the catering for the August houseparties at All Hallows, Rousdon. Roger was very impressed with the way that she handled the job and invited her to become Lady Warden at Lee Abbey, but she did not accept. After having served in the army during the war, and then being involved in relief work in Germany, she did not feel at all keen about the idea of living in a community. However, Roger was not the sort of person to take 'no' for an answer. A year and a half later he was still asking her to come as Lady Warden. In the end she agreed to come for six months, until they could find somebody else. She was to stay for twenty-eight years!

Another important arrival along with Madeleine and Jack in the spring of 1948 was a herd of nine cows. In fact eight had been expected, but one had calved on the way! They formed the nucleus of the Lee Abbey farm and their purchase marked a significant policy decision for the Council. After careful consideration they had decided that it would be right to farm the estate commercially. It was a brave step, for it involved taking out a further loan of £3,000 on top of the loans already outstanding on the original purchase of the building.

In the same way as Nehemiah rebuilt the walls of Jerusalem, or the Lord had called on St Francis to rebuild the church of San Damiano, the physical work needed to restore the Lee Abbey building and estate was a visual parable of the work of God through the Community in rebuilding his Church. There was much rubbish and debris which had to be cleared away; there were parts that had fallen into disuse which had to be restored to their former purpose; there were areas that needed radical alteration in order to meet current needs, and above all the full potential of all that God had provided needed to be discovered and put to use. The task of Lee Abbey was to encourage the Church to realise the full potential of the resources offered to it by Christ; to discover the power of God to change people's lives and equip them for service. The Church possessed tremendous resources in its membership, which it did not know how to use. Part of the vision of Lee Abbey was to provide the training to discover and develop the ministry of lay people, in a Church where it was too often felt that ministry was the province of the professional clergy.

Together with the building, the Trustees had purchased 350 acres of land. About 190 acres of this was woodland; a further 60 acres, consisting of the former golf course around the house and Crockpits (the headland beyond Lee Bay) was capable of cultivation. The remaining 100 acres at Caffyns Down, which had formed a second golf course, was an entirely separate unit which was sold off in 1951.

The only part of the estate which had been consistently maintained was the vegetable garden behind the main house and a walled garden with two glasshouses. These had provided a valuable supply of fruit and vegetables for the school. With rationing still a major problem, these gardens continued to be an important source of food for the Community and guests.

Squire Bailey had laid out the main part of the estate in the last century. Woodland was planted with Sessile oaks, and a network of paths was constructed through the woods and along the coast. After twenty-five years of neglect the woodlands presented a major problem. An enormous amount of work had to be done to hack through the undergrowth and reclaim the paths, clearing out many of the trees that came down in the gales each year. Then, as now, they provided a more than adequate supply of logs for use in the house, and were even a useful additional source of income. If the character of the woods was to be maintained for future generations, then a large amount of thinning out and replanting was necessary.

Another obvious way of augmenting the food supply was to keep livestock. Pop looked after a number of chickens and ducks down at Lower Lodge, and there were a couple of pigs. The first two pigs – Gert and Daisy – proved to be a great success and so were succeeded by Bits and Bobs. Stewed rabbit was also a very familiar item on the menu of most of the early houseparties.

The first cows were Welsh Blacks, a very hardy breed that could live off the rough pasture, and stay outside throughout the winter. The farm buildings were very rudimentary, and for milking, the cows would be tethered to a row of posts outside and, of course, milked by hand. If it were raining then you got more milk! Their milk was extremely rich and the guests greatly appreciated the plentiful bowls of clotted cream. It was only as the land improved that these Welsh Blacks were replaced by Ayrshires.

All this initial work of clearing the woods and establishing the farm was supervised by the first estate manager, John Ellis, until he left the Community to prepare for ordination. However, the work would never have been done without a great deal of outside help, especially from the student working parties. These have been arranged since 1946, and have played a crucial part in maintaining the estate. Until 1995 two week-long working parties were held during the Easter vacation, and students came and spent part of their time working and the rest sharing in normal houseparty activities. Some medical students from Birmingham, a couple of parish youth clubs, and a group from Exeter University were among those who came in 1947, but particular links developed with Oxford and Cambridge Universities. Both pastorates welcomed the evangelistic ministry of Lee Abbey as complementary to their own work. The clear message of the epilogues, presenting the claims of Christ and the challenge of personal commitment, provided direct teaching without narrowness.

The experience which the working parties offered, of being able to work alongside the Community, and so share more deeply in the life of the place, was to have a profound influence in many lives. However, now changing patterns of student life are necessitating changes in the format of the working parties. The semester system means that students are no longer as available in the Easter vacation. A more flexible programme of working parties is emerging involving both students and others who are willing to come to work on the estate and these are being spread throughout the year.

News of the great things that God was doing in North Devon soon began to spread as guests returned home full of all that they had experienced. Of those whose

lives were changed by Christ at Lee Abbey during those
early years, probably none was to become better known
at the time than Dr Jim Bell-Nichol. He was a GP and
became a regular contributor to a very popular radio
programme called *The Silver Lining*.

It was the first week of April in 1947, and rather
reluctantly, he had been persuaded by a friend to go
with his family and stay at Lee Abbey for a much-
needed break. He knew a little about the nature of
the place, but he was, as he put it, 'prepared to put
up with a modicum of religion for the sake of a pleasant environment'. However, each evening he attended
the epilogue, even though there was no compulsion
to do so.

Early one morning challenged by the epilogue of the
previous evening, he went to the chapel and began
to pray, using the mnemonic PSALM that had been
presented in the epilogue. As he later wrote

P for praise. I was full of gratitude to God for
so many things that P was easy. What's next? S
for surrender. S for surrender. I could not go on.
It was a complete blank wall as regards prayer.
Either no prayer or S for surrender. I had thought
about it in the night but had decided it would be a
good thing to carry out at some future date, maybe
when I went home, and then I wouldn't have to
tell people at the epilogues. Most embarrassing.
Meantime S for surrender – I hesitated long. I
knew only too well what surrender meant for me.
Then quite deliberately I said to God, 'O Lord,
I surrender, and if there is anything I have not
surrendered, help me to see that and give it to
Thee also.'

With his surrender to Christ, Jim found healing from
agoraphobia – a fear of open spaces – which had developed from experiencing shock as an eighteen-year-old

soldier in the First World War. Leaving the chapel he walked along the path to the cliff edge at Jenny's Leap and prayed 'God take this thing away from me'. 'I can best describe what happened next by saying it was as though I had taken off a heavy overcoat on a summer's day. In a few moments my heart stopped thumping – my breathing became natural – my mouth became moist. I was a free man. I knew in an instant that the spectre had vanished. I remember singing at the top of my voice as I completed my journey to the sea'.

Two years later, Dr Jim gave his testimony on a radio service broadcast from Lee Abbey, but he was unable to use his own voice, for he had developed multiple sclerosis, a progressive type of paralysis. Yet this crippling disease in no way caused him to regret that surrender of his life to Christ. In that broadcast, he referred to himself as 'the happiest man in England today'. He found many ways of ministering to people through his broadcasts and his writing. He was a frequent visitor to houseparties, and God gave him a very special ministry to many people before his death in 1954.

It would be a most unusual houseparty – and cause for considerable concern – if the final epilogue on the Friday night did not include a number of people like Dr Jim who shared with the Community and their fellow guests their new-found faith in Christ. Perhaps even more significant than these testimonies were the letters which came to members of the Community, when guests, with their holiday well in the past, shared their excitement, joys and frustrations as they discovered the reality of the living Christ in their home situations.

God was honouring the faith of the founders and was blessing the work of Lee Abbey. It was not that they had discovered a neat evangelistic technique. There were those who, not having visited Lee Abbey, were suspicious that it was practising evangelism by pressure. It was easy to assume that unsuspecting people were being lured to so-called 'holidays' to be, in fact, subjected either to directly aggressive or more subtle psychological pressure to become Christians. A visit to Lee Abbey would quickly establish that this was very far from the truth. Although each houseparty always had a programme of sessions, discussions and nightly epilogues, it was made very clear that nothing was compulsory, and, as now, there was no disapproval of those who choose to do other things. The only pressure felt at Lee Abbey is the pressure of the Holy Spirit convicting a person from within; no one is approached with any 'hard-sell' evangelistic strategy.

It is not possible to analyse neatly the means that the Lord uses to touch people at Lee Abbey. Different guests testify to different things. Yet in the end, the majority comment that it is 'somehow the atmosphere of the whole place'. Many remark that they are struck by this as soon as they arrive. There is something different, but they can't put their finger on it. This can also have an adverse effect. There is a story of one girl from a family with no Christian background, who was coming down to the Youth Camp held each year in August. Her parents brought her down by car, and as they passed through the gateway at the Top Lodge, her father commented upon the atmosphere. By the time they had driven a few hundred yards further along the road to the Entrance Tower, he could stand it no longer. He told his daughter to get out of the car, gave her her luggage and suggested that she walked the rest of the way down the hill. He turned the car round and drove away at top speed.

The sheer beauty of the setting makes a profound effect. 'The heavens declare the glory of God' is a ready response to anyone watching a dramatic sunset over Lee Bay, or admiring the variety of views from Duty Point Tower.

Many guests are also struck by the friendliness of both fellow guests and Community. If their previous experience of Christians has been either of a formal, cold gathering or of false heartiness, then the natural friendliness of very normal people can be a great surprise. Witnessing the life of the Community, not merely when they are talking about Christianity but going about their daily work, makes a powerful impression, especially on those for whom the Church has been seen as a building rather than as a fellowship of people.

The nightly epilogues and morning sessions also made a great impact on many who came to Lee Abbey in those days. For many guests, it was the first time that they had heard the Christian faith simply explained and related to the needs of the modern world. Here indeed was good news for those who had previously seen Christianity in terms of the obligation of church attendance and of good works, with no idea of being able to enter into a personal relationship with God. Each week the epilogues would follow the same basic theme, looking in turn at man's need, God's answer in Christ, and the power of the Holy Spirit. As well as the talks, epilogues would often include short testimonies from different members of the Community and guests, in which they would share something of how they had come to know Christ, and were experiencing Him at work in their lives. These testimonies, often very nervously given, would speak to people as powerfully as the main talk, for here were ordinary people who demonstrated that it was no theoretical Christ that was being offered.

Whatever means the Lord used to speak to those who came, crucial to all that was going on was the undergirding prayer. There was the daily worship of the Community; the houseparty team, comprised of both Community and guests, would meet each day after breakfast to plan and pray for the day's activities; a group of people prayed each night during the epilogue for the speaker and for those who were listening: and there were the prayers of the Lee Abbey Friends, people from all over the country who had committed themselves to pray for the work. If Lee Abbey is in the end about the work of God rather than the work of man, then indeed it is this prayer which is the key to all that happens.

Lee Abbey was to have a greater impact on those from overseas than on any other group of people. Since the first houseparty season in 1946 it had been decided that an International Houseparty should be a feature of the programme. Yet these houseparties were far from easy.

As the guests gathered for the International Houseparty at the end of August in 1947 wartime attitudes and tension were very evident. The atmosphere was distinctly cold, as many people began to realise exactly who had accepted the invitation to the houseparty. As well as those from England there were groups from France, Holland, Germany and Switzerland. For the Dutch and the French it was the first time since the war that they had met any Germans. On the third evening, during the epilogue one of the Germans stood up and asked if he might speak. 'I was a leader in the Nazi Youth. Now I am a Christian. I ask that you accept my apologies for all that my people did to your people during the war. Please forgive us.'

That apology, not merely the fact that forgiveness had been sought but that it was given, transformed the houseparty. As the fortnight progressed each person began to discover what they thought was impossible, how in Christ their natural hatred and prejudice could be overcome as they shared and worshipped together.

The Community had discovered another very important element of the ministry that God had for them: to be a place of reconciliation, where individuals and groups can discover what it means to both forgive and to be forgiven for acts that often go back many years.

Links between Lee Abbey and churches on the Continent continued to grow. The closeness of the links that developed between Lee Abbey and Holland resulted in the visit of Princess Wilhelmina to a houseparty in 1951. During the war she had been Queen of the Netherlands but had abdicated in favour of her daughter. Not even in the days of old Squire Bailey had Lynton seen anything quite like this!

A Dutch pastor had indicated that if the Community were to invite the Princess to visit, she would probably accept, as she was very interested in all she had heard about Lee Abbey. The invitation was sent, but apart from a formal acknowledgement from her secretary, nothing further was heard. Then quite unexpectedly came the news that she was planning to come for a week in September! The house was already fully booked and was not really furnished for royalty, but she decided that she would stay at the Tors Hotel in Lynmouth and come out each day to Lee Abbey. The local taxi, 'Bod', was pressed into service, and with the driver in peaked cap and white gloves, the Princess and her lady-in-waiting drove through Lynton to Lee Abbey. On the final day of the houseparty she attended the Communion service in the octagonal lounge, to receive Holy Communion in the Anglican Church for the first time. At the final epilogue she asked if she might speak:

I will not forget what I have learned in your Community. I was glad to experience the spirit of brotherhood and understanding among us all. It is wonderful to see how all differences, everything vanishes before the living Christ and our unity in Him becomes real, a unity manifested in having intercommunion.

When we go back to our duties and our homes, let us tell all who are willing to work for Christ, to make sure that what they are planning for, or have planned, fits in with His plan, for rescuing mankind out of the entanglement of today.

A pine tree planted by the Princess in the field in the front of the house is a reminder of a very memorable visit by someone who was felt by all to be a very gracious Christian.

* * *

Lee Abbey was clearly a place that the Lord was blessing, but few guests realised that behind the scenes things were far from easy. When the auditors were asked to prepare the financial accounts for 1947–8, to be presented to the Council of Management, it became clear that there was considerable administrative confusion. It was necessary to distinguish between the work of Lee Abbey for which the Council was responsible, and other ventures organised by Roger under the name of Pathfinder, such as external houseparties and publishing. Roger was anxious to push forward and implement his ideas, while the Council was increasingly anxious to make sure that Lee Abbey was based on a sound footing.

If the devil could not frustrate the work from outside, he was certainly trying to undermine it from within. When a new member is admitted to full membership of the Lee Abbey Community he is now asked this question, 'Are you prepared to live in fellowship, being open to be known for what we are, accepting one another in Christ, and saying of others nothing that could not be said to them personally if love and wisdom required it?' This question is included in the Community promises out of the experience that it is in the area of relationships that the Community is most vulnerable. During 1948 and 1949 there had been an increasing breakdown of relationships within the senior Community at Lee Abbey. At the Council meeting on March 10th 1950, Roger offered his resignation as Warden of Lee Abbey and it was accepted.

Chapter 4
Serving the Church

'You had better send in to me any names that come to you and I will shortlist them,' suggested Geoffrey Rogers, chairman of the Lee Abbey Council. They were discussing the crucial question of the appointment of the new Warden. It was going to take some time to get used to the idea of Lee Abbey without Roger de Pemberton. Indeed there were some people who questioned whether it could survive without his drive and enthusiasm. It was Roger to whom the Lord had given the initial vision and it was he who had gathered round him those who were to implement it. It was essential that his successor should be a person who shared that same vision for evangelism and the renewal of the Church.

It was early on a Monday morning – closing day for sending in the nominations. Geoffrey and Dora were still in bed when Dora suddenly said, 'What if somebody suggests you?'. It was the first time that the possibility had occurred to either of them, but now the idea suddenly gripped them. Geoffrey got out of bed and went to kneel beside Dora. Together they prayed that the Lord would guide them and show them His way.

When Geoffrey arrived in his office at CMS Headquarters in Salisbury Square his secretary pointed out five letters, each marked 'Confidential', waiting on his desk. All the letters were brief. Each in turn had only one name to suggest, 'Geoffrey Rogers'.

His appointment was confirmed at the next meeting

of the Council in April. Roger had agreed to remain at Lee Abbey until the end of the summer season and so on Michaelmas Day, September 29th 1950, Geoffrey was installed as the second Warden of Lee Abbey, a post he was to hold for the next fourteen years.

Geoffrey had been brought up in Cambridge where he went to school and university. During his first term as an undergraduate at St Catherine's College, he met the children's evangelist, Hudson Pope. Many years before, this same man had been used by God to bring the young Leslie Sutton to faith in Christ. Geoffrey had been asked by his mother to take his younger sisters to a CSSM meeting in a house just outside the city. He was asked in by the hostess, felt too embarrassed to refuse and so heard the Gospel explained and began to wonder about its relevance to his life. His curiosity aroused, he went to further meetings until finally he committed his life to Christ.

There was plenty to encourage a young Christian in Cambridge, and it was not long before he began to sense that God was calling him to the ordained ministry. After taking his degree he went to theological college at Ridley Hall to prepare for ordination. Not having moved from Cambridge he was able to keep close links with many of his university friends and was introduced to Dora Howden, a young undergraduate from Girton College with whom he promptly fell in love.

On being ordained deacon in 1927 he went as assistant curate to St James', Gravesend, while Dora remained in Cambridge to complete her degree. After only two years at Gravesend, Geoffrey went out as a missionary to Persia with CMS. Dora joined him two years later and they were married in Isfahan. By 1939 they were due to come home on furlough. They arrived back in England in February but the outbreak of war made it impossible for them to return. With their future very uncertain, CMS appointed

Geoffrey to their Headquarters' Staff and he became Candidates Secretary. Like all missionaries he was expected to do his share of deputation work – speaking in parishes about the work of the Society and the needs of the Church overseas. It was this that took him, in July 1943, to speak at the annual missionary meeting in Cuthbert Bardsley's parish in Woolwich. Cuthbert was very impressed by Geoffrey's concern for evangelism and invited him to take part in a Holy Week mission the following year. Another member of that mission team was Jack Winslow, so for the first time Geoffrey heard of Lee Abbey and about the plans to purchase the building in Devon. Geoffrey already knew Roger de Pemberton; they had been contemporaries at Cambridge. He was excited by the vision for evangelism that the Lee Abbey project offered and so, with his experience in Iran and his connections with CMS Headquarters, he was an obvious person to become one of the seven Trustees.

A new phase in the story of Lee Abbey began with Geoffrey's arrival as Warden in September 1950. The traumas of the early years were to be followed by a long period of stability, in which all that had been pioneered was set on a firmer footing and consolidated. God had brought together three men to lead the second stage of Lee Abbey's ministry.

Geoffrey, Leslie and Jack came to be known as the 'Three Musketeers' as they led the Community over the next ten years. It was an unlikely trio: they were very different in temperament, background and age. Each had first-hand missionary experience but they came from very different spiritual positions although they shared a common passion for evangelism. Together they formed a powerful team.

Geoffrey, as Warden, was very much the leader, although the youngest of the three – ten years junior to Leslie and twenty years to Jack. Full of energy, it seemed he could turn his hand to anything. He took a keen practical interest in the working of the estate; he found great delight in driving a tractor during the student working parties, and he would always go to bed with his wellingtons and torch nearby should one of the diesel generators need attention in the night. An enthusiastic pianist and singer, he would take responsibility for the training of the choir for the tableau on Christmas Eve each year, auditioning every new, highly nervous Community member!

There were some of his friends who felt that by coming to Lee Abbey, with stoles, candles and links with Anglo-Catholics, Geoffrey must have abandoned his conservative evangelical position. It was the time when evangelicals in the Church of England were very suspicious of other traditions. Yet anyone who heard Geoffrey speak could have no doubt of his evangelical convictions, with his clear, simple presentation of the Gospel and his stress on the need for personal conversion by repentance and commitment to Christ. Lee Abbey stressed 'Christmanship' rather than 'churchmanship' and Geoffrey wholeheartedly welcomed this approach. As time progressed the experience of working with people like Jack enabled him to appreciate and value other traditions, though for a long time some people felt that he was rather cautious about the Catholic and the sacramental aspects.

Leslie Sutton was every bit as warm-hearted as Geoffrey, yet his role in the Community was very different. He was still suffering the effects of his wounding in Gallipoli; severe headaches were a recurring problem and at times this meant that he was not always easy to work with. His stammer meant that he could be almost inarticulate yet the message got across as he hammered away at the great truths he had learned: the need for adventurous faith in God and to experience the power of the Holy Spirit.

For some, his very direct evangelistic technique was rather overpowering, as he would quite literally collar someone, grasping them by the shoulder. Yet this was the approach which God used to reach those who would have avoided any less direct challenge. As the layman of the three, his contribution at Lee Abbey demonstrated to clergy and laity alike that spiritual ministry is not the sole preserve of ordained clergy.

The third member of the triumvirate, Jack Winslow, was different again. His presence ensured that Lee Abbey could not be labelled simply 'evangelical'. He brought with him a wealth of spirituality from his Anglo-Catholic background and time in India. His age and style of life meant that he was the father-confessor figure in the Community in both the formal and informal sense. His daily quiet time – an unhurried time of prayer and reflection at the beginning of the day – was of prime importance to Jack, both in his teaching and in his personal life. Nobody was quite sure what time he got up each day, but it must have been around 5.30 a.m. Yet early rising also meant an early bedtime and at ten o'clock whatever else might be happening, Jack would make it clear that the time had arrived for him to retire to bed.

While he was an undergraduate at Oxford Jack had heard the American evangelist, John R Mott, speaking about 'the morning watch' and so began a practice that he was to continue for the rest of his life. Writing in his book *When I Awake* (published by Hodder in 1957), he says,

> I can now confidently say, if in these years I have been able to accomplish any useful service to God or man, I owe it to no other single cause so much as to the habit then started of keeping the morning watch. My experience over these years has taught me that this quiet hour spent with God day by day is an unfailing secret of power, progress, purpose and peace.

The way he spent this quiet time evolved over the years. His reading of Christian mystics, like Lady Julian of Norwich, together with his experience of Indian mysticism, brought new dimensions to his prayer and Bible reading. The Oxford Group had added a further strand. Its teaching laid great stress on the need to spend a time each day waiting on God to receive divine guidance about every decision of daily life. This was seen as coming both through the reading of the Scriptures and also, with one's mind concentrated on God, waiting for direction. In later years the Oxford Group was to receive justified criticism of this practice which could cause people to misinterpret their own whims as being the guidance of God, sometimes with distressing consequences. Yet for Jack this waiting upon God was rooted in his prayer life and study of the Bible, and became a source of daily strength in living a life which was each day surrendered to God.

Geoffrey and Leslie were equally insistent both in their teaching and by their own personal example, that anyone who wanted to take the Christian life seriously, must spend time alone with God each day. It was expected of the Community; the Community promises included the question, 'Have you accepted the discipline of regular private recollection through Bible reading and daily prayer?' Four things were considered essential for the young Christian at Lee Abbey – a Bible, notepad, pen and alarm clock! The most compelling feature of Jack's teaching about the quiet time was that his life was evidence of the supreme worth of what he was saying.

Whilst Geoffrey was a musician, Jack was a poet, writing many poems and hymns, including some that have become popular such as 'Lord of Creation, to you be all praise', and 'Come sing the praise of Jesus' sung to the tune of the Battle Hymn of the Republic. He was also an accomplished author, producing a steady stream of popular books, including the first *Lee Abbey Story*.

These three men provided the Community with a leadership that was clearly authoritarian but deeply respected. It would be wrong to assume that relationships were always easy, but the key to their unity was their commitment to team-work – the style of working propounded by the Oxford Group. This was not an easy way to choose. They had to make themselves vulnerable if they were to be fully open with each other. In this way, as they discussed and prayed together, a deep trust developed. Even when they disagreed, they were able to accept Geoffrey's ultimate decision as Warden.

They were three great men of faith and the task which they undertook required no less faith than had the initial establishment of Lee Abbey. Indeed in some ways it required more, as they began to explore ways of recognising and developing the full potential of the work.

The Community itself offered great possibilities: here was the greatest resource for evangelism that Lee Abbey had been given. The deeper the commitment of the Community to Christ and to each other, the more effective would be its witness. However, it was not easy to establish and maintain a depth of commitment when the membership of the Community was constantly changing and it was known that many people's involvement was only for a limited time. The recruitment of suitably mature Christians willing to stay for some time was clearly essential. Even more crucial was the need to set up a community structure which would encourage Christian growth. To this end the significance of red and green name badges, denoting full and probationary members, was established. It was decided that Community promises should be made in two stages. After one month at Lee Abbey people became associate members and after six months they could ask to be received into full membership, assenting to a series of searching promises.

The same basic principles of membership still apply, although periodic reviews have simplified the wording and caused less differentiation between short- and long-term members. There is now one set of Community promises in the form of seven questions. They are:

1. Do you affirm before the Community your personal faith in Christ and your desire through prayer, study and service to seek a deep and mature faith?
2. Do you understand by this that your mind, your time, your talents, your possessions and all your relationships are to be increasingly surrendered to Christ as Lord?
3. Do you promise to be loyal to the Community in its aims, its work, its standards of behaviour and its disciplines?
4. Are you prepared to learn to live in fellowship, being open to be known for what we are, accepting one another in Christ, and saying of others nothing that could not be said to them personally if love and wisdom required it?
5. Have you accepted the discipline of regular private recollection through Bible reading and daily prayer?
6. Do you intend to make the weekly corporate Communion the central act of your work and worship?
7. Are you ready to serve, in every way, those who come to us, seeking to help one another to a clearer and deeper knowledge of Christ, through your work and by your words?

The first three are taken on arrival, when a new member receives a green name label. They are retaken together with the remaining four promises after a probationary period of at least three months, when a person becomes a full member of the Community and receives a red label. All Community members restate their Commitment annually at the Community Quiet Day in Holy Week.

Changes to deepen the commitment of the Community included the introduction of a system of allowances. Initially certain members of Community had been paid a salary, although when money was very short many of them had been willing to forego pay completely. It was agreed that all Community members, irrespective of their jobs, should be paid the same small allowance in addition to receiving their board and lodging. A scale of increments according to length of service is now provided, but the principle is that people are paid according to their need rather than as a reward for service. As the majority of Community members stay at Lee Abbey for only a limited time, it has always been important for members to maintain some financial independence, and so no common pooling of money has ever been considered.

With the deepening of the discipleship of the Community came the development of the Friends – those people, who generally had stayed as guests and shared Lee Abbey's vision for evangelism and renewal. The fellowship of Lee Abbey Friends was established almost from the beginning. It had a twofold purpose; to encourage the prayer support and financial backing that was essential for the maintenance of the work, and also to provide follow-up support and encouragement to those who had been to houseparties.

Here was another great potential to be realised, not only for Lee Abbey but as a spiritual fighting force throughout the country. To try to dispel the image that a Friend was someone who supported a building, the title was changed from Friends of Lee Abbey to Lee Abbey Friends of Jesus. A simple admission service was introduced during the final evensong of each houseparty, and Friends were asked to renew this commitment each year. It stated that Friends were those who: 'have committed themselves personally to Christ the Saviour and Lord; are prepared to work through prayer and witness for the conversion of others; pray regularly for the renewal of the Church, for the work of Lee Abbey and for the other Friends'.

A real danger that faces any Christian centre like Lee Abbey is that people will see it as an alternative to their local church. The stated purpose of the Community has always been that it exists to support local churches. Guests at Lee Abbey are constantly encouraged to be fully involved with and committed to their local congregation even if they find that to be difficult and discouraging.

This concern that Lee Abbey was called by God to support the local church meant that from the beginning there was a particular ministry to clergy. *Towards the Conversion of England* had pinpointed the need for the English clergy, traditionally seen as pastors, to be trained for evangelism, and other concerns were also noted. It was a time when many were still on such pitifully small incomes that families who desperately needed a holiday from their parishes could never afford to take one. Then there were clergy who, having been in a post for a number of years, had become overtired, disheartened at the apparent lack of success and had lost much of their spiritual vision. As if this were not enough there were depressing trends in the Church; dwindling congregations, lack of manpower necessitating the amalgamation of parishes, and the general questioning of the role of the parish priest which had hitherto been unchallenged.

Within the first eight years it was estimated that over 1,000 clergy had stayed at Lee Abbey. They came for varied reasons but from the beginning there were those who were eager to be involved with Lee Abbey and its work.

As finance was so often a crippling problem for clergy families, the team decided that it would be right to

invite, free of charge, a number of clergy with their
wives to a clergy recess in the week following the
Easter houseparty – a good time for parochial clergy to
take a break. This was another venture of faith, for the
Community still needed as much money as possible to
help clear the debts. Yet during the week itself a Friend
who knew nothing of what was happening wrote saying
that she felt guided to send a gift to Lee Abbey and
enclosed a cheque for £200, sufficient to cover the whole
cost of the week. Similar provision was to be made the
following year. These clergy recesses became an annual
event, and it was later necessary to run two successive
weeks to cope with the demand.

They were by no means easy times and some of the
clergy were far from sympathetic with what they found
at Lee Abbey. The visit of one clergyman, however, was
to be remembered by the Community for many years.
On returning home after a clergy recess he telephoned
the Community to tell them that he had been greeted
by his daughter with 'Mummy, Daddy's come home
with a new face!' A little girl's exclamation was able
to explain what God had been doing far more clearly
than any sermon. Her father, Arthur, was a curate
in Ilfracombe. An invitation to a recess had been sent
to his vicar. He, being rather suspicious of Lee Abbey,
had deputed his curate to go in his place. The opening
session had already begun as Arthur arrived at Lee
Abbey and his worst fears were soon confirmed: as
he sat at the back of the octagonal lounge his face
betrayed the fact that he was far from happy. Yet
as the week progressed he found that his suspicions
were allayed by the atmosphere of warm fellowship.
The party differences that had once been so prominent
in his thinking became minor considerations in the
light of the new relationship with God that he was
experiencing. He returned home a changed man and
it was to influence the whole of his ministry.

With such a diverse group of clergy it might have

been assumed that speakers would have to be careful in what they said. Yet there was no soft pedalling; what mattered was commitment to Christ. The continual stress was on the need for the Church to present a strong evangelistic message and to preach the necessity for personal conversion. It was inevitable that such an approach would receive a mixed reception, not only because of its theology, but because the clergy were challenged to consider their own commitment to Christ. One couple made their feelings very apparent by refusing to come into epilogues. As everybody settled down in the octagonal lounge, they would sit and read their newspapers in the small lounge. For three successive years they came to the recess without attending any talks, but gradually something was stirring within them. One night they propped the door open, and then it was noticed that they had moved and were sitting in the corridor just outside, surreptitiously listening to all that was being said. At the end of their third visit, as the couple were driving off, the wife suddenly wound down the car window and handed a note to Geoffrey, who was saying farewell to the guests. Quickly she wound the window up again and they drove away. The note read, 'I want to let you know that last night I gave my life to Christ. I went down onto the beach at Wringcliffe Bay and baptized myself in the stream that runs over the sand.'

It was to be the beginning of a whole new ministry for both of them.

Clergy, whose work calls them to offer help to others, are often the most reluctant to accept help for themselves. This has meant that some of the most outstanding clergy weeks have also, at times, been the most difficult. On several visits as guest speaker Agnes Sanford introduced the subject of the healing of memories and a few years later Frank Lake, with the subject of clinical theology, was helping clergy to understand themselves as a way of enriching their counselling ministries; for many this was a painful exercise.

Equally controversial, though in a different way, was the decision to invite Methodist ministers to join with the Anglicans for a joint recess in the autumn of 1965. The Anglican-Methodist unity commission had just been set up. There was a great disappointment and frustration when the Bishop of Exeter stated that he would not give permission for the Methodist ministers to join in Holy Communion at the conference. Lee Abbey's practice of admitting non-Anglicans at Holy Communion had always been regarded with considerable suspicion in the Diocese. It seemed that the only answer to this problem would be to have no Communion services during the week, but merely an *agape* meal at the end. This was most unsatisfactory, for it caused Lee Abbey to emphasise the very disunity that it was seeking to heal. The Bishop subsequently rescinded his ruling, and granted permission for responsible members of the other Churches to join in Holy Communion at Lee Abbey whenever a conference was specifically aimed towards reunion. Although the numbers at that particular recess were disappointingly small, it was an important breakthrough for the Diocese of Exeter. It seems extraordinary on reflection to note that it was not until 1968 that Methodist clergy were regularly invited to join in clergy recesses, and it was another three years before clergy of other denominations were finally included!

However, by this time the recesses had become only a shadow of their former selves. With the rise of a whole variety of conferences for clergy, an invitation to stay at Lee Abbey was no longer a great attraction. Only one recess was held each year, and even this was often difficult to fill. Popular speakers would still draw larger numbers, but the Community had to realise that the needs of the clergy had changed: Lee Abbey's ministry to them had to change accordingly.

Today a steady stream of clergy continues to come to Lee Abbey, to houseparties, conferences and mid-week breaks. The most pressing need of many is for a holiday with their families, and special rates are offered to help make this possible. Others are seeking a time for spiritual reflection, which is less structured than a traditional retreat.

Many ministers first visit Lee Abbey when they are still training at theological college. Since 1950 the Ordinands Conference, normally held in the first week of January, has been an annual event. It is a unique conference in that all the Anglican theological colleges are invited to send representatives, and this is now extended to the Roman Catholic and Free Church colleges. The Community saw this ministry to ordinands as being at the very centre of the vision of Lee Abbey, and great care was taken to issue invitations and make the conference known. As with the clergy recesses, the early conferences were often far from easy. Many ordinands came with deep suspicions of other traditions, which were not lightly shed. It seemed as if some were there because they had been sent, rather than by their own choice, and at one time it was considered unwise to indicate a person's college on his name badge! Yet this meeting together was invaluable. For some ordinands it was the first time that they had met and talked with someone from another tradition, and many came to appreciate others' insights. One practical repercussion was a request from the students to their college principals to begin an exchange scheme whereby several students would exchange colleges for a couple of weeks.

The mood of the Ordinands Conference has altered over the years. With just as many colleges represented, there is now a much greater warmth and little sign of the previous sense of suspicion. As many ordinands are now married with young families as they undertake their training there is a much greater family emphasis to the Conference.

For a number of Community members a time spent at Lee Abbey has been a preparation for ordained ministry. One such former member of the Community described his time at Lee Abbey thus, 'I was like a very battered ship coming into dry dock, being scraped down and refurbished with new engines and new oil and then being launched slowly'. David had first come to Lee Abbey on a student working party in 1954. Three years later, after going through a bad period of depression, he returned as a working guest. His month's stay did not produce the immediate change for which he had been longing and so the time was extended. It was only after six months as a working guest that he felt able to accept the suggestion that he might become a member of the Community. For the next two years he worked with Ursula on the farm looking after the poultry. Slowly the experience of living in the Community, knowing the love and the care of the Body of Christ surrounding him, together with wise counselling from Jack, Leslie and Phyllis and also prayer when hands were laid on him, were to bring David the healing that he was seeking. He was also to discover that the Lord was giving him a ministry of healing, but it was not until his last couple of months that the idea of ordination became a real possibility to him. After being accepted for training he left the Community to spend six months working in Coventry before going to theological college. He was to be the fourth man in succession of those responsible for the poultry at Lee Abbey who went on to be ordained!

A number of clergy have returned with groups from their parishes and this ministry has emerged as one of the most significant parts of Lee Abbey's work. Often it is only when a group from a church go away together that they begin to relate to each other. Barriers come down as the churchwarden is discovered in

his dressing-gown collecting his early morning tea at
7.30 a.m., or a member of the youth group is faced by
an elderly spinster in a dance in which neither is quite
sure of the steps! It is not merely that Lee Abbey offers
suitable accommodation where a group can stay; what
is more important is that a group is able to witness
the life of a Christian community. Small details of
Lee Abbey's daily life can leave big impressions. The
fact that the accountant, not the chaplain, is leading
evening worship; the evident care and support from
fellow Community members for the highly nervous girl
giving her testimony; the natural unity of a Baptist
and high Anglican as they lead a pre-breakfast Bible
study. For many groups, observing the way that the
Community works raises big questions about their own
life together.

Worshipping with the Community may also be a new
experience. The limited space of the chapel means that
on Sundays the octagonal lounge is the setting for
the main morning worship, normally a Communion
service. The form of service, and even the music may
be familiar, though a full room with good acoustics –
the octagonal lounge was built as a music room – does
aid singing. With the table in the centre of the room, a
circular seating pattern means that people are facing
their fellow worshippers, rather than staring at the
back of their heads. They are not merely told they are
the Body of Christ, many are able to experience that in
a new way.

In this way many parish groups are given new
insight into worship, and return to seek ways of implementing what they have experienced in their own
churches. This is true for many individuals who stay
at Lee Abbey but they can often face frustration,
when, on returning home, their enthusiasm is met
with indifference or even hostility. It can be very
different for a group especially if it includes clergy
and church leaders such as PCC members, and there

are many churches for whom a group visit to Lee Abbey has been significant in their spiritual growth. This has become one of the most significant parts of the Lee Abbey programme and the number of weekends set aside for church groups has grown steadily. Through them God continues to use Lee Abbey to bless and renew not just individuals but congregations.

Chapter 5
Under the Shadow of His Wings

'Where God guides, He also provides' is a familiar saying, and in retrospect the history of Lee Abbey is a powerful testimony to its truth. Yet the fact that God really is faithful in keeping His promises is often discovered slowly and painfully, and only with the realisation that faith is itself a gift of the Holy Spirit. God has promised to provide what we need rather than what we desire. If we ask, we will receive, though it may not be either in the way or with the timing that we had assumed. One reason is that God's vision is often so much grander than man's. Few of those involved in the founding of Lee Abbey in the 1940s would have imagined that it could have grown to the size and position that it has in the 1990s.

The history of Lee Abbey is rich in incidents where God has dramatically and spectacularly demonstrated His power both to provide and to protect. Such stories strengthen us, perhaps coming as a rebuke to our lack of faith, by reminding us that God really does answer prayer. However, one cannot pretend that there are not also stories of disappointment where a prayer, offered in faith, has not been answered in the way that was confidently expected. Such disappointments are often only to be tempered in the light of future events when God's true purposes are seen.

God's greatest provision at Lee Abbey is people. Time after time God has called just the right people to fill vacant places on the Community. Experience shows that God does know Lee Abbey's needs. Yet there have been times when manpower has seemed lacking, and God's word to the Community has been to discover within the existing members previously unrecognised talents, be it for cooking, milking cows or counselling somebody in deep distress.

God's hand has been seen continually in the financial provision for the work. Lee Abbey was managed on a shoestring, and financial needs were not kept a secret – indeed the shortage of money was apparent to any who came to stay. It was not unknown for the payment of Community allowances to depend on the receipts from the toll road. Often urgent needs have been met through gifts of money or goods from guests.

One typical situation was faced by the Community in 1948. The previous summer had seen fewer guests than planned, and was followed by a winter period during which the Community received virtually no income. By June nearly £2,000 was owing to tradespeople in the Lynton area. Leslie had witnessed similar situations before, in WEC, and he felt very strongly that this should not be allowed to continue: it was dishonouring to God. He was determined that by the end of the month God wanted these debts to be cleared, and so specific prayer was offered that the Lord would provide £2,000 by the end of the month. Leslie added a postscript to his prayer. 'Lord, may it come in large sums, so that we don't have to write too many receipts!' Midway through the month a piece of paper was pushed into Leslie's breast pocket as he stood talking to a guest in the octagonal lounge. Absent-mindedly he pushed his spectacles on top of it and did not find it until the next morning. It was a cheque for £1,000. Those on the Community, who were aware of the situation, thanked God for this cheque and confidently waited for Him to provide the other £1,000. Yet it was not until the very last day, June 30th, that another cheque was received, again for £1,000.

The prayer had indeed been answered, and only two receipts were written!

Yet at the same time as this most direct answer to prayer there was a great disappointment. In May Lee Abbey had undertaken its biggest publicity exercise yet. A glossy brochure entitled *Counter Attack* had been produced. It set out in stirring language the vision for evangelism in Britain that lay behind the work of Lee Abbey.

> We believe and expect great response in prayer, interest, gifts of money and legacies, and full co-operation in making the work and its needs widely known. Will you stand together with us in faith and prayer – regular prayer that all God's purposes for this work may be fulfilled; will you get quiet with God and see if He wants you to give in any way to this work? We ask only for that help which you believe is guided of God.

Yet God apparently did not guide. Fifteen thousand copies were sent out to both clergy and laity, yet the only visible response was a handful of encouraging letters and about £120. It was a monumental flop, and an expensive one, at a time when Lee Abbey could not afford it. The prayers of the Friends had been sought through the newsletter to back this distribution, but God had clearly shown that financial needs were not to be met in this way.

However, the Lord was not allowing Lee Abbey to run at a deficit. Each year the giving of the Lee Abbey Friends and other donations meant that the accounts could show a small excess of income over expenditure. Yet, the mortgage had hardly been reduced at all in the first five years. In 1950 there was still over £25,000 outstanding, costing nearly £1,000 a year in interest. An appeal was made through the newsletter for offers of interest-free and low-interest loans. Sufficient offers of loans came in, and so a debenture issue was made possible. An unexpected source of income came when it was discovered that Caffyns Down (the unused 100 acres of land) could be sold for three times its estimated value!

From 1952, each year saw a significant reduction in the outstanding debt of £20,000. By 1955 only £2,545 remained to be paid off. That year marked the tenth anniversary of the founding of Lee Abbey and it was decided to mark the occasion by moving the annual London reunion service, normally held in St Martin-in-the-Fields, to St Paul's Cathedral. To some it seemed a very ambitious vision but over 3,000 Lee Abbey Friends and guests packed the cathedral for the great service of thanksgiving. The day was to be a landmark in the history of God's provision for Lee Abbey. It had been decided that the collection at St Paul's should go towards the clearing of the debt.

In preparation for the service Geoffrey explained to the head verger that a large collection of over £1,000 was anticipated. 'Sir, a collection in four figures would be a record for St Paul's Cathedral.' Geoffrey's warning was not heeded, for the collection plates and alms dish proved totally inadequate for the amount of money, with pound notes spilling over onto the floor.

The established pattern for the reunion day was that, after the Thanksgiving Service during the first part of the afternoon, everybody would move to the Central Hall, Westminster to renew friendships over tea and join in the more informal rally. The rally was well in progress when a telephone call came through from St Paul's to say that the collection was £2,055. Only £490 remained to clear the debt. Cuthbert Bardsley, the chairman of the Council, put the challenge to the assembled Friends. A time of quiet was kept, and then the collection bags were passed round. Later he announced the total. It was £1,153. Everybody stood and sang: 'Praise God from whom all blessings flow!'

In ten years over £40,000 had been given for the establishment of Lee Abbey. The next year saw another repercussion from that day, when a conference for vergers was held at Lee Abbey!

However, the provision of money is not the only way that God chooses to show His care for His people. From the beginning it was obvious that a chapel would be essential at Lee Abbey, to provide both a room for services, and also a place of quiet for Community and guests. There was not really much choice about where it should be. After the octagonal lounge and the dining room, the next largest room in the house was one on the first floor that had originally been Squire Bailey's bedroom. It was a beautiful light room with a magnificent view over the estate, and dominated by an enormous mirror. The one drawback was that it could seat only about forty people in comfort which meant that two services of Holy Communion were held each Sunday morning and still many guests would find themselves sitting out on the landing trying to join in the service through the open door. The situation was not helped by the fact that the room was adjacent to a whole line of bathrooms and toilets with their customary noises!

The only option was to build, and in 1951 the Council took the decision to build a new chapel on the North Lawn. It was to be built of local stone, and would cost £5,000. At this time there was still a large amount of money to be repaid on the debt, but it was felt that Friends would readily respond to the appeal. But God had other ideas about how this need was to be met. After the war the extreme shortage of building material meant that a licence was necessary for the construction of any new church building. The money for the project was beginning to come in, but it became clear that Lee Abbey would not be granted a permit for the project. The only possibility for a new chapel would be if some modification could take place within the existing building.

A new estate manager, Geoffrey Hutchison, had just been appointed and as he and Geoffrey Rogers walked around the buildings an idea came to them. They noticed that on the north side of the house between the two main chimney stacks were three bedrooms. Closer investigation confirmed that these rooms were merely divided by partition walls which had no structural significance. The walls and the ceilings could be removed, and the three bedrooms, together with the passageway, would create one large room with windows on both sides; the ceiling would run up church-fashion into the roof, and it would be capable of seating about 100 people.

What is more, one room was on a slightly different level from the other two, which meant that there was already an inbuilt chancel step in exactly the right place!

Once the necessary permission had been granted it took only a few days for a very enthusiastic group of students to do the necessary demolition work – throwing the rubble out of the windows onto the North Lawn – and disconnecting the old iron radiators and central heating pipes. A local builder did the plastering and Leslie worked on the carpentry with the Community. A few weeks later, at 7.00 a.m. on Easter Day, Geoffrey celebrated Holy Communion in the new chapel for the first time. In a fraction of the time and at virtually no cost God had provided Lee Abbey with a new chapel.

God often chooses to meet the needs of His people in this way. What we assume can only be achieved by much work and at great expense, is often already ours if only we will recognise it and use it. The plans for the new building were not abandoned, but set aside, as it was not impossible that God might one day call Lee Abbey to go ahead with this major building project.

Other new building has taken place over the years. Desperately needed single rooms were provided in 1955 with the building of twelve single annexes at the back of the main house. In 1957 Garden Lodge was built to provide accommodation for the Warden and his family, separate from the main building. The twenty-first anniversary was marked in 1967 with a further building project. This included a new service road at the back of the house, so that goods vehicles no longer had to drive round the front of the house to reach the yard, and a new bedroom block with twelve single guest rooms, a playroom and laundry for guests. Another long-cherished vision came to fruition in 1974 when the new kitchen, constructed in the inner courtyard, was completed. This work was done mainly by Community members with a small band of local workmen, and so was completed at about half the estimated contract price. The new kitchen enabled the dining room to be enlarged, and the canteen area to be constructed.

Special gifts came in for all these projects, yet in many ways they were part of the natural development of Lee Abbey, in step with the general improvement in living standards throughout the country.

The Community had come to accept with humble gratitude that it was not unusual for a guest to want to make a gift to Lee Abbey, to thank God for what he had received. In 1967 it became known that someone wanted to make a substantial gift: his one condition was that he should remain anonymous. He came to be referred to affectionately as 'Ben', for benefactor. It was generally believed that the gift was in thanksgiving to God for the conversion to Christ of two of his children at the Youth Camp. The form of the gift was not to offer a specific sum, but to make money available for any project that would make Lee Abbey more self-sufficient by improving the facilities of the estate, like food production, the water supply and storage of fuel. It was to be up to Lee Abbey to suggest how this might be done and to submit proposals to him.

The decision was made to ask for a replacement for

the antiquated cowshed and dairy and to construct a purpose-built farm. This was exactly the sort of project that 'Ben' had in mind. A new building would mean that it would be possible to enlarge the herd, provide modern milking machinery and generally increase the efficiency of the whole farm. John Burkett, the architect who had designed the new bedroom block, was asked to draw up plans which were submitted both to the Ministry of Agriculture and also to 'Ben'.

The new farm was built on the site of the old guest car park and came into use in the autumn of 1969. The herd was now almost doubled in size and the cows could be much more efficiently milked and fed. The total value of the gift to Lee Abbey was nearly £18,000.

No description of the ways in which God has provided and still provides for the needs of Lee Abbey would be complete without writing about water. Lee Abbey's remote position means that it has always depended on its own water supply from a number of springs in the hillside above the house. This water is exceptionally pure, and beautiful to drink, but on several occasions, when faced with a very real possibility that the supply might fail, the Community has been reminded that it is not to be taken for granted. In the early years it also relied on this water supply to generate its electricity.

Nearly every summer Lee Abbey would face the same problem. By August, when the house was at its busiest with the holiday fortnights and the Youth Camp, the number of those living on the estate would be almost doubled, and the level of water in the tanks would fall dangerously low.

Guests became accustomed to the ban on baths and the red ribbons that Madeleine tied onto cistern handles as a reminder that they should only be flushed if absolutely necessary! For Lee Abbey water was a precious gift from God.

Twice a water diviner had been called in. On both

occasions water was detected but it was a very long way down, and digging and blasting failed to get through the solid rock to reach it. This was not God's solution to the problem.

The water situation reached a crisis point at the end of the long dry summer of 1972. It had now become vital to the running of the house for the water supply to be increased. As the Community prayed, it was almost reminiscent of the Children of Israel in the wilderness crying out to the Lord for water and complaining 'Is the Lord with us or not?'

At this time there was a party of students from Ewell Technical College staying in the house, and they were helping Jack Usher, the engineer, move some of the plastic water-piping higher up the hillside. It was while they were doing this that one of them slipped and dislodged a stone at the side of one of the streams. They noticed that the ground was quite muddy. The next day as Jack dug around the area, a new spring, strong and clear, came bubbling out of the bank. It did not take long to get the water tested, and within twenty-four hours of its being connected to the main supply, the water tanks were again filled to overflowing. 'Usher's gusher', as it came to be called, supplied all the water needs of Lee Abbey throughout the seventies, so that even in the very dry summer of 1976 there was no shortage at all. The Sisters of Mary from Darmstadt in Germany gave Lee Abbey a number of slate plaques to be positioned on the estate. One of them was to go above this spring. It reads:

> O sing to the Lord a new song,
> For He has done marvellous things!
> His right hand and His Holy arm
> Have gotten Him the victory.

This spring in turn was to prove inadequate, though it continues to provide water to the Beach Chalet and

Pelton House. In 1990, two and a half acres of land with a good spring were purchased from Six Acre farm, and the Community continues to take water from the Ram overflow at Six Acre.

* * *

On many occasions the Community has been aware of God's protection. Exmoor must be one of the most beautiful places in England, yet, when the wind howls across the moor and lashes the sea against the rocks, or when the mist descends, it can quickly become one of the most desolate and wild places in this country. Anyone who lives in Lynton or Lynmouth will know that the weather is not a force to be trifled with, but a power very much in the hands of God.

As so often seems to happen in August, the weather for the first holiday fortnight in 1952 had been very dismal. It seemed to have been raining nearly the whole time and the last day, Friday, August 15th, was certainly no exception. In fact the rain was coming down even harder. In the house it was a matter of keeping the children occupied and doing the packing, but down at the Youth Camp life was not so easy. Many of the tents were leaking and much of the ground in the sleeping area was under water. If the strong winds continued, much of the night would have to be spent holding the tents down. So after a hurried supper it was decided that the girls should go and sleep in the café on the beach, and all the boys should be moved into the big marquee which was on slightly higher ground.

Elsie Savill, the accountant on the Community, also acted as the quartermaster of the camp. Together with David Cole, another member of the Community, she had gone up to the main house to get some dry bedding and make things as comfortable as possible for the girls sleeping on the floor of the café. With the girls safely transferred, the Camp Commandant, Raymond Scantlebury, had informal prayers with them and then returned up the road to the main camp field. By this time, Elsie's tent had begun to leak and she decided that she would go and sleep in her own bed up at the house. The car was parked on the road outside the camp field, and David Cole offered to carry her wet bedding for her. He went on ahead as she laced up the door of her tent.

As soon as David stepped out of the camp field, he found himself swept away by a raging torrent. The road had turned into a fast-flowing river, as the normally gentle stream had burst its bank. It was only by grabbing an old gate post by the Pelton house, fifty yards on, that he was able to stop himself being swept out into the sea. With the tremendous sound of the wind and the rain, Elsie did not hear David's shouts, and as she stepped out of the field she too was swept off her feet, but after being dragged over the stones and rocks for a few yards she was able to get to her feet and clamber out of the water. Struggling to the bank they made their way up to the house to tell Geoffrey what was happening. He telephoned the police who told him that in Lynton they were facing an even greater crisis.

Meanwhile, despite the storm raging outside, the girls at the café had gone to sleep while two members of the team took it in turn to keep watch. About 3.00 a.m. they looked out to see that the water was now lapping within an inch and a half of the back door. Together they prayed that the Lord would protect them, and when they next looked out, they saw that the water was now beginning to subside. It was not until the next morning that they discovered what had happened.

As soon as it was light Geoffrey woke Madeleine and together they went down to the camp. The boys had spent the entire night holding down the tents and they were all safe. Where the road had been, there was now a massive ten-foot hole, and the only way of reaching the girls at the café was to go across the field and scramble down the bank. The girls were all safe – indeed, many of them commented that they had had a very good night's sleep! Not far from the café lay a great tree trunk which had been swept down by the torrent and had been jammed against the sides of the bank. It was probably only this tree that had deflected the course of the new river. If it had not been there, the torrent might have swept straight through the café, almost certainly destroying it and killing many people.

On the Saturday morning, the guests in the house and many of the campers were due to go home. After the events of the previous night it seemed very unlikely that they would be able to get through. A visit to Lynton confirmed that indeed all the roads in the area were blocked, if not washed away. Lynmouth was completely sealed off by the Army, and it was clear that something terrible had happened.

At 10.00 a.m. an Army dispatch rider arrived at Lee Abbey to say that three coaches would be coming in half an hour to pick up all the guests and the campers. One half of the road at Barbrook had been reopened, and the Army was anxious to get all visitors out of the area as quickly as possible. Lynton and Lynmouth faced a severe health hazard, with the drains and mains water supply badly damaged and electricity cut off. Lee Abbey, with its own water and electricity, was virtually the only place in the area functioning normally that day.

Gradually, the full horror of what had happened that night became apparent. Nearly nine inches of rain had fallen on Exmoor in less than twenty-four hours. The moorland streams which fed the East and West Lyn rivers had turned into raging torrents carrying with them a great mass of boulders and trees. The swollen watercourse swept through Barbrook, and destroyed the entire centre of Lynmouth with its hotels, chapel and harbour. Thirty-four people lost their lives. When

Harold Macmillan, then Minister of Housing, visited the area, he commented that the scene reminded him of the First World War battlefield at Ypres.

Madeleine tried to see if there were any ways in which the Community could help the flood victims, but it seemed that the WVS and the Red Cross had everything well under control and there was little that could be done. On the following Sunday 'Pop' was leading the service at Barbrook Church for which Lee Abbey was responsible at that time. In the congregation as usual was Tom Floyd, a postman from Lynmouth. He had lost six members of his family in the floods, including his wife, one son and one daughter. Tom's faithful dog, Tim, came with him to the service and never let his master out of his sight, even following him around the church as he took the collection.

Apart from the damage to the dams, and the loss of the road to the beach, the Lee Abbey estate and all who were staying there that night, were completely unharmed by this terrible disaster. A few days after the flood, a national newspaper published an aerial photograph of some tents with a caption describing the makeshift accommodation of the flood victims. It was in fact a picture of the Lee Abbey Youth Camp!

A disaster like this always causes people to question how a loving God can possibly allow such a horrific thing to happen. Why should some die and others be spared? It is one of the eternal mysteries to which the Christian can produce no simple solution. For Lee Abbey, the event was a very humbling reminder of the Lord's protection when faced by potential catastrophe.

Twice, the estate has been threatened by fire. It was the first day of the Easter houseparty in 1956 when a fire began in the Valley of Rocks and advanced rapidly towards the estate. Fire brigades from miles around were called in to battle against the great walls of flame. As on all occasions of crisis, Leslie Sutton gathered together a group of people to pray that the fire might in no way harm the estate.

Only a few weeks previously the junior chaplain, Ken Pillar, had been married to Margaret. Top Lodge, which stands at the entrance of the estate, was their first home. As the fire was advancing the fire officer told them that they would have to evacuate the house, and so with a number of the Community they began to move everything out, stacking all their possessions along the side of the road. But even as people were passing things out of the upstairs windows to load them onto the trailer, down below Leslie was carrying them back in again through the front door, announcing that they must have faith! The time came when the Fire Officer said that it would no longer be safe to go back into the house; but suddenly the wind changed direction and the flames began to move away from Lee Abbey and up the hillside. It was an incredible sight for there was a semi-circle of flames around the south-east of the estate, but at no point did the fire come on to Lee Abbey property.

Similar scenes were witnessed three years later, although this time it was the main house that was threatened. A group of Community members were returning along the cliff path from Lynton, after a long walk on Exmoor, when they saw smoke and flames coming from the cliff side ahead of them. Their immediate thought was that it was Lee Abbey itself which was on fire, and it seemed that no one was aware of what was happening. Quickly the alarm was raised, and it was discovered that a fire was already well out of control along the cliff to the north of the house.

Some young boys who had been fishing at Lee Stone had started a fire to cook their fish, but had not completely extinguished it. The summer of 1959 had been very dry, and by September all the vegetation was parched. The tremendous heat produced by the fire was causing an updraught that was in turn drawing the flames up the cliff side. All the able-bodied men of the Community and guests helped the firemen tackle a very difficult situation. There was no way of getting water to the area and the only method of containing the fire was by beating and hacking away at the undergrowth in front of it.

The situation was becoming increasingly serious. When the fire reached the path at the top of the cliff it would then be in the woods. From there, once it got hold of the tops of the trees it would quickly spread to the main house. The house was evacuated and the firemen played their hoses on to the trees surrounding the north lawn and the roof of the house to try to prevent any sparks from taking hold.

Once again it was to be Leslie, the man of faith, who rallied everyone to prayer. All those who were not involved in the actual fire-fighting were summoned to the north lawn. Leslie led them in prayer that God would change the direction of the wind and would protect the house from harm. They looked up to see that the sparks were blowing not towards the house, but out to sea. The next day the Chief Fire Inspector commented, 'I don't have any particular faith, but it was a miracle that saved your building'. The progress of the fire had been halted by an increase in the off-shore wind, just as the flames had reached the top of the cliff.

Although it was possible for the guests now to return to their beds, that was not to be the end of the danger. The cliffs smouldered for over a week, and a constant watch was kept by the Community men day and night, to put out any small fires that flared up. In the very dry conditions the fire smouldered deep in the undergrowth, and quite unexpectedly a gorse bush would suddenly flare up. It was not until the rain came that they could be certain that there was no danger of another outbreak.

Thus Lee Abbey was spared from fire on two occasions. There is nothing remarkable about variations in the strength and direction of the wind, which changes all the time; but on both occasions the merciful alteration came at a critical moment, and when people were praying.

Not long after the Lynmouth flood disaster, there was yet another incident that clearly demonstrated God's protecting hand on Lee Abbey.

From the beginning there had been problems with the roof of the octagonal lounge. Every time it rained, a whole collection of buckets would be needed to catch the drips. Something had to be done. It was decided that the lounge should be re-roofed – the pitch of the roof should be increased, the lead taken off and replaced with felting. To do this involved removing the boarding, which revealed the main skeleton structure of roof timbers.

One Saturday morning while this work was in progress, Geoffrey and Dora were preparing to go to a meeting in Lynton in connection with the flood disaster. They had just got into the car when Geoffrey felt a strange compulsion that for some reason he must go and look at the work being done on the roof. So, dressed as he was, he ran upstairs, climbed out through the window that led on to the roof and saw that the workmen were in the process of replacing the boarding. As he looked more closely he saw that the roof was constructed out of two massive beams that spanned the entire room, and on which all the other timbers rested. In horror he noticed that in one place, one of these beams had rotted virtually the whole way through and was in danger of collapsing at any time. Already late for his meeting and with Dora waiting in the car, Geoffrey could not stay any longer so he gave hasty instructions to the workmen that they must find the foreman and do no more work at all on the roof until he returned.

With the meeting over, Geoffrey immediately went back up on to the roof to see what should be done.

He found that his instructions had been ignored and the boarding replaced. This time he was able to make sure that the repairs were effected; the boarding was removed again and the rotten beams made safe.

Of the three Musketeers, Geoffrey was probably the one least accustomed to acting on impulse, yet had he not obeyed his inner prompting to inspect the roof, Lee Abbey might well have been the scene of a most terrible tragedy had the roof collapsed on a room filled with people.

Chapter 6
Turbulent Times

Is Lee Abbey a place in North Devon, a community of people, or a movement within the Church?

This question has been debated many times and it was in the background of much of the discussion in the Lee Abbey Council during the fifties. The issue was whether God was calling the Council to establish centres in other parts of the country to extend the work of the original vision.

Once the work in Devon had become securely established the Council no longer had to spend all their time on the administrative details, which had been essential in the early years. So while continuing to keep a close watch on all that was happening they were able to explore other possibilities. Some members of the Council were anxious that Lee Abbey should proliferate – a house near Lynton being but one of the many centres that they might establish.

Two ideas were debated at the Annual Council Conference in January 1953. They were the establishment of a training centre, and 'a London house'. The majority of Lee Abbey guests came from the Home Counties, and a need that was continually being voiced was for a Lee Abbey centre in London itself. Clearly it would be supported. The monthly meetings held at the Royal Empire Society in the winter months were attracting up to 500 people to listen to challenging messages from speakers like Cuthbert Bardsley and Wallace Bird. If there were a permanent centre, it could become a rallying point for Lee Abbey Friends, a place for planning and prayer, and a base for training. The idea was very attractive. It was also a real possibility, as two properties, which appeared to be most suitable for these purposes, had been offered to the Council.

After investigation neither property proved to be right. The Council continued to explore the idea of setting up a training centre and over the next few years a number of enquiries were made and several places visited, yet none was suitable.

There were also plenty of people who were eager to see the establishment of other places doing similar work to that of Lee Abbey in Devon, running holiday houseparties. A number of the Council, including Geoffrey, were very cautious of this. Although it was clear that God was richly blessing the work in Devon, there was no guarantee that a similar venture in another part of the country would be successful. It was a complex series of factors that God had brought together; there were the Community, the leadership, and the beauty of the setting, and none of this could be duplicated automatically in another place.

The strongest move for another Lee Abbey came from the North of England. As early as June 1948 Jack had written in the newsletter that 'I have always thought that some place similar to Lee Abbey must in due course be established somewhere in the North, to meet the needs of those who can hardly be expected to come all the way to Devon from there'. The Council did not then feel it right to take any active steps to investigate this possibility. In 1957, a group of Lee Abbey Friends from the North took the initiative to circulate some 700 Friends in that area asking for their response to the possibility of 'founding in the North an instrument for the revival of the Church, perhaps a Community of the same general character as Lee Abbey'.

From the strength of the replies they decided actively to pursue this idea. Already a possible property had been discovered. A Lee Abbey Friend, Bernard Jacob, was taking part in a mission at Skipton. Talking to his hosts about Lee Abbey and his longing to see such a place in the North of England, his attention was drawn to a nearby property that was being advertised for sale, Scargill House, situated near the village of Kettlewell in Wharfedale.

The initial reaction of the Council was not favourable to the proposal. The team at Lee Abbey did not feel it was worth the journey to visit the house; it was too small to be economic, and was situated in the wrong place. They were to change their minds when they saw the beautiful location for themselves.

Events moved much more swiftly than the Council had envisaged, and in November an agreement was signed at Middleton Rectory in Manchester by a small group, chaired by Donald Coggan, Bishop of Bradford, to purchase Scargill House. As in the purchase of Lee Abbey it was a great act of faith; the group had committed themselves to raising £20,000 in gifts or loans – within two months.

With the decision taken, the Lee Abbey Council were anxious to support the venture in every way possible, though realising that they were not to be responsible for the work, as they had initially assumed. A letter was sent out to all the Lee Abbey Friends with news of the new scheme and explaining the financial needs. It received a remarkable response. Within the two months, over £42,000 had been offered as gifts or as loans; a sufficient sum both to purchase the property and to enlarge and equip the house.

Although Scargill has always been totally independent of Lee Abbey, the close spiritual affinity that exists between the two communities was demonstrated at the official Dedication on June 27th 1959, which was conducted by Cuthbert Bardsley, Bishop of Coventry and chairman of the Lee Abbey Council. A visitor to Scargill, having stayed at Lee Abbey, may soon observe that whilst the pattern of life and ministry adopted by the Scargill Community reflects a number of features pioneered at Lee Abbey, there are a number of notable differences. For example, the idea of the team or Chapter, which has always been considered to be the heart of Lee Abbey's administration, has never been adopted at Scargill. Also, being situated close to the heart of industrial England, near Leeds and Bradford, Scargill has been able to establish from the beginning a special ministry to industrial and secular groups.

When Scargill was opened, Lee Abbey had been established for fourteen years and was clearly enjoying considerable success. Guests were flocking to house-parties and many applicants had to be disappointed; the work was now based on a sound financial footing. Money was not plentiful, but neither was it a problem; the policy was to keep the fees as low as possible while still covering running expenses. Behind the work was the concerned backing of a large company of Friends.

The atmosphere within the Church of England had also greatly changed. The fifties had been a time of encouragement, highlighted by the visits of Billy Graham. His methods were inevitably controversial, yet he managed to reach the general public of the country with the Gospel, in a way that no church or individual had managed to do for many years. The great crusades at Harringey in London made a profound impact on the Church. Some people wished to dismiss the crusades as being based purely on emotionalism, but time proved otherwise. The crusades engendered a new sense of urgency and enthusiasm in many clergy and lay people for evangelism. Many regular church attenders found themselves 'converted' and now living as evangelical Christians in non-evangelical and often anti-evangelical churches. For the Church of England the lasting impact of the crusades was the number of men who, tracing the beginning of their spiritual life to the crusades, later offered themselves for ordination. Many people whose lives had been touched at the crusades visited Lee Abbey to find teaching and encouragement. No longer could the Community feel alone in the work of seeking to promote evangelism within the Church of England.

This renewed concern for evangelism meant that Lee Abbey was becoming far more acceptable within the establishment of the Church, compared with the times when it was either unknown or aroused considerable suspicion. No less than five members of the Council were bishops. At the annual thanksgiving service in 1960, Geoffrey Fisher, Archbishop of Canterbury, was present. The words that he spoke in St Paul's Cathedral before he gave the blessing, demonstrated to the Community and to the Church Lee Abbey's acceptance within the establishment.

I have for long included Lee Abbey among the works of the Church for which I praise God; and I have praised Him with increasing certainty and happiness as time has gone on. Today I have seen something of your spirit and of your fellowship. I have received from you new refreshment and encouragement in the service of the Lord, from your numbers here gathered, from your voices raised in prayer and praise. I praise the Lord with you, have magnified His name together with you. I shall be able now with even greater sincerity and confidence to thank God for you, your witness and your work.

Here was the evidence that God had honoured the faith of the founders, as Lee Abbey enjoyed spiritual and material success. But it was a situation that was fraught with danger. Lee Abbey was born as a venture of faith, but now there was no longer the need for the daring faith which had to depend on God alone for material and spiritual needs. The pioneering days were over and there was a temptation to see the task as maintaining a proven system and style of ministry. Leslie, in particular, sensed the danger of complacency. In his message to the Friends at the start of the new decade he wrote, 'Though we humbly thank God for all His blessings since 1945, we are terribly aware that we, the Lee Abbey Friends, need a new vision and an anointing of the fire of God's love if ever we are to meet in any degree the challenge of the world's desperate need in 1960.'

After a time of great stability at Lee Abbey, the new decade was to bring a time of much change. In 1960 the ministry of the Three Musketeers, who had been at the heart of Lee Abbey for the last ten years, was drawing to a close.

In 1958 Leslie had suffered a severe coronary thrombosis, and had been in Barnstaple Hospital for three months. Although he made a good recovery it was clear to both him and Phyllis that their time on the Community was limited and that they should be seeking a less demanding ministry. Jack was 78, and although still very active, thinking nothing of leading a 23-mile Doone Valley walk, would clearly not be able to continue much longer.

Over the years the chaplaincy team had been built up, so that it was now customary to have two younger ordained men on the Community in addition to Jack. This team was further supplemented by the arrival of the first woman chaplain, Kristeen MacNair.

Later that same year, 1960, Leslie and Phyllis were offered a flat in Farnborough and retired from Lee Abbey to continue an active ministry together, especially among Lee Abbey Friends, until Leslie's death in 1968. They were succeeded by Gordon and Sheila Mayo and their family, who had just returned to England after spending ten years working with the Christian Council in Kenya. These replacements among the team and other senior Community members inevitably brought change; new people were able to look at Lee Abbey through different eyes and spark off new ideas.

As a direct result there was considerable debate about the nature and the purpose of the Community. Until 1960 the position had never been questioned. Lee Abbey had been founded as a centre for lay training and evangelism; the purpose of the Community was to serve the guests – without the guests, the Community had no significance.

Now several people, like Kristeen and Gordon and Sheila, felt that the Community should be seen as having significance in itself. After different experiences of community life overseas they were attracted to Lee Abbey partly by the exciting possibilities of further exploring the Christian life in a community. They believed that Lee Abbey, in addition to its ministry to guests, was an important experiment by God, which had much to teach the whole Church.

This subject was discussed at length both in the team and in Community meetings. There was a tendency to reduce the debate to a straight choice between two contrasting positions. Was Lee Abbey a 'guest house' staffed by resident members, living as a community, or a Christian community which opened its doors to share its life and home with other people? This over-simplification seemed to sum up the difference between the first and second generation at Lee Abbey. Geoffrey, as one of the founders, was anxious that the place should not become introspective, preoccupied with itself, and so lose its cutting edge as an agent of mission. For others the mission of Lee Abbey consisted not merely in what it said or did, but in what it was, and there was a danger of being so preoccupied with activity centred around the guests, that the life of the Community suffered.

It was a debate that produced no clear-cut solution; rather it highlighted a healthy tension, with which the Community continues to live. The problem is not unique to Lee Abbey but has to be faced by any community that is essentially 'task orientated' and indeed by any local church congregation. Has God placed us in a certain situation 'to be' or 'to do'? A balanced Christian life will have to hold these two together.

The debate about the nature of the Community was nothing compared to the great debates that were shaking the whole Church of England at this time. For the Church the sixties was a deeply disturbing decade. Throughout society it was an age of questioning and searching. Authority was being challenged in a way that had not been experienced before and the Church was not to escape.

As Billy Graham had become a household name in the fifties, in the sixties, it was John Robinson, Bishop of Woolwich who attracted enormous publicity, mainly through his book *Honest to God* which was published in 1963. John Robinson's thinking was really a strange amalgam of bits of two incompatible theologians, Dietrich Bonhoeffer and Paul Tillich, but in his questioning of what he made to appear to be somewhat tired Christian convention, he somehow caught and articulated a restlessness which was present in the culture of his time. He did seem to strike a chord for a number of his contemporaries. For many ordinary church people the whole situation was bewildering. It appeared that the foundations on which their faith was laid were being questioned by the Church itself – the existence of a personal God, the historical facts of the life of Jesus Christ, the authority of the Bible as the Word of God. For a number of Christians, this requirement to think out what had always been assumed was refreshing and strengthening; for many others it had exactly the opposite effect. Perhaps hardest hit by the whole radical theology debate was evangelism – the very validity of which was, for some, in question. The vast publicity given to the views of the radical theologians meant that many non-Christians were only too aware of the confusion being experienced within the Church, and would summarily dismiss a simple evangelistic approach appealing to the authority of the Bible and the work and life of Jesus. How should Lee Abbey respond?

There was no doubt in the minds of Geoffrey and Jack that this new theology was not the message that God had entrusted to Lee Abbey. Jack wrote in the editorial of *Christian Witness* in September 1963, 'It is a strange delusion that so anaemic a Gospel, emptied of its life blood, can be "the power of God unto Salvation" for modern man. In an age of astounding miracles it is already outdated. In an age of tempestuous doubt it offers soundings of no sure anchorage. In an age of deep and widespread spiritual hunger it offers a stone for bread.'

It was not possible simply to ignore what was happening, and continue with the well-proved approach, just waiting for this phase to pass. Groups such as ordinands, sixth-formers and students demanded that the issues were faced. Geoffrey's epilogue on Personal Relationships, for example, was no longer receiving unchallenged acceptance. The 'PR' talk, though the subject was really sexuality and boy–girl relations, had become a regular feature of many houseparties, especially those involving young people. Now, the so-called 'new morality' and situational ethics, which made love rather than law the criterion for moral decision-making, meant that Geoffrey's traditional conservative approach would be openly questioned.

While Lee Abbey was having to face these issues, the Council again had the important task of finding God's choice for a man to be Warden. At the January meeting in 1964, Geoffrey announced that as he was soon to be 60 he felt it was time for him and Dora to move on. The previous few years had not been easy, either within the Community or in the wider Church, and he felt that a younger man was needed to lead Lee Abbey. As with Roger de

Pemberton's departure in 1950, many people were going to find it very strange to think of Lee Abbey without Geoffrey – the place was so much identified with him.

At the end of the houseparty season in October 1964, Geoffrey and Dora moved to take up the post of Canon Missioner in the Coventry Diocese. It was a memorable departure. On their last day at Lee Abbey it was already dusk by the time they were finally ready to go. There was hardly anybody around as they said farewell to Madeleine in the yard and quietly slipped away. Then as their car turned out of the entrance tower they saw that the road to the Valley of the Rocks was lined by Community members carrying torches. As the car passed, each person followed it until the whole Community was gathered at the head of the Valley of the Rocks. They had no doubt that they were marking the end of an era.

It is not easy to find the right person to follow a man who has been successful and popular. Geoffrey had clearly been God's man for Lee Abbey in the fifties, and now different qualities were needed in the man who could work out the vision in the sixties. Change would be essential, if Lee Abbey were to continue to speak to the Church.

The man chosen was Ken Pillar, vicar of St Mary Bredin, Canterbury. For the Council, Ken's appointment had one great advantage; he had served as chaplain at Lee Abbey for five years under Geoffrey. They were looking for change, not merely a continuation of Geoffrey's ministry, and in Ken they were confident that he would know what he was changing.

Ken's links with Lee Abbey went right back to the first houseparty season. While on leave from the Navy he had been intrigued to read of the new venture in North Devon and so had come to a houseparty. He was deeply impressed by all that he experienced that week and became a regular visitor, first as a student from Cambridge bringing friends to working parties, and then as a curate from Liverpool. When it was decided to appoint a junior chaplain he had been an obvious choice. So after an absence of seven years Ken and Margaret, with their four young children, moved back to Lee Abbey; on January 25th 1965 he was installed as the third Warden.

As expected, the Community soon discovered that Ken's style of leadership was very different from Geoffrey's. They had lost a father and gained an older brother. Ken knew that he was not the omni-competent leader to which the Community had become accustomed.

There was a significant relaxation of Community discipline. For example, the weekly corporate communion service was put back half an hour to begin at 6.30 a.m. Rules that forbade men to visit the girls' rooms were lifted, and a very thorny issue was finally resolved when it was decided that tennis and putting could be played on Sundays, a question that had been debated at great length by the Council.

What was happening at Lee Abbey was no different from what was occurring in universities, colleges and similar institutions throughout the country – a swing towards greater freedom, more general involvement in decision-making and away from strict discipline.

Ken also brought a new theological approach to the ministry at Lee Abbey. Like Geoffrey he was a convinced evangelical, insisting on the need for personal conversion and commitment to Christ, yet he was noticeably more liberal in his approach. Although he would disagree with much of what the radical theologians like John Robinson were saying, he was anxious that they should not be dismissed out of hand. People needed to listen carefully to what they were trying to say before passing judgement. Greater openness became a feature of the houseparty programmes. Guests were encouraged to learn from each other in small discussion groups. Epilogues became shorter, covering a greater variety of subjects than the clear-cut pattern of the fifties which had looked in turn at God, Man, Sin and the Cross leading to the challenge evening. Speakers would talk openly about doubts and uncertainties as well as convictions. It was inevitable that some guests, familiar with Lee Abbey under Geoffrey Rogers, would find the changes disturbing. A correspondent to the *Church of England Newspaper* wrote, about a recent visit to Lee Abbey:

> One could not avoid the realisation of some of the currents flowing within the Community and I have no reason to doubt the accuracy of reports from respected Christian friends who went on other houseparties recently. They speak of Christians leaving in utter distress. What is the evangelistic impact of a place where the leading members of the Community seem unworried by the fact that they contradict each other openly upon matters of basic importance . . .
>
> Some have always been dubious about Lee Abbey's attempt to make an appeal to all sections of the Church of England. I have always hoped that it would succeed, and I believe it still could. But it is a delicate tightrope to walk if a real evangelistic balance is to be maintained . . . [Referring to Cuthbert Bardsley's impending retirement from the Council:] one fears that his departure from the Chairmanship could be an omen of doom to this endeavour, which as you rightly say, has for twenty-two years had a tremendous influence for good in the Church of England.

This theological tension came to a head in the student working parties. For almost twenty years the Oxford and Cambridge University pastorates had been bringing groups of students together to the spring working parties. The two pastorates are very different in structure and organisation, and in the sixties they represented two distinct theological positions and approaches to evangelism. The Oxford pastorate, based at St Aldate's Church, was traditional in approach, seeing its task as evangelism and the nurturing of young Christians. The Cambridge pastorate was much more loosely structured, involving a number of college chaplains and including a radical element, with a strong intellectual emphasis.

As the two groups came together each spring the Community witnessed in microcosm what was happening in the Church. The main point of friction was the content of the evening epilogues by the pastorate chaplains. Each side was deeply disturbed by the approach of the other. While the sympathies of the majority of the Community were probably with Oxford, the Chapter was anxious to remain impartial, believing that it was good for the groups to come together. They sensed that in the daily team meetings they were witnessing not merely a difference in theology, albeit a major one, but a failure in communication, with neither side listening to the other. In 1968 the two groups decided that it would be better if they came to separate working parties. It was a solution to a long-standing tension but it was accepted by the Community with great sadness. The one consolation was that both groups were still willing to maintain their links with Lee Abbey.

This whole dispute was very much a product of its time. In later years the situation was to be completely different, the two pastorates continuing to come on separate weeks but with a deep spiritual bond developing between them.

Chapter 7
Lee Abbey in London

Jack had been reading the recently published *Life of St Francis* by Elizabeth Goudge. At the weekly team meeting, he shared with the senior members of the Community something that had caught his imagination. This was the description of the 'Chapter of Mats' held at Assisi in 1219.

Francis had preached on a minstrel's chant;

> Great things we have promised,
> But greater are promised to us.
> What we have promised let us fulfil,
> To what we are promised let us look forward.
> A brief delight and punishment forever;
> A little suffering and glory infinite.

Jack saw the obvious implications that this had for Lee Abbey, and he proposed that there should be a 'Chapter of Friends', a calling together of the Lee Abbey Friends, just like the early Franciscans, to wait upon God and seek His will for the future.

Both the team at Lee Abbey and the Council welcomed Jack's proposal and detailed plans were laid for the Chapter to be held at Lee Abbey from September 9th to 16th, 1961. The plan was to bring together some 500 Friends, most of whom would have to be accommodated in guest houses and hotels in and around Lynton. Jack stated that the purpose of the week was to renew the spiritual life of the whole company of Friends, lifting it to a higher level and also to see if God was challenging them to new action.

> May we not hope that, just as the Chapter of Mats led the Franciscans to new and more daring adventures for Christ, so at our Chapter of Friends God may call us to some new enterprise, some further outreach, which will encounter any temptation to rest upon our oars, and enable us to be of wider service to God, to the work of his Kingdom?

In preparation for the Chapter, Friends were asked to write in with new ideas of how they believed God might be leading Lee Abbey and the Friends. There was a ready response. Friends were involved in a wide variety of Christian and secular service, and here was the opportunity to relate that to Lee Abbey. A number of common themes emerged. There was the desire to find an expression of deeper commitment to Christ. Could Lee Abbey establish a 'third Order'? What about lay training? Lee Abbey was a centre for evangelism and lay training, but many felt the lay training aspect was hardly touched upon.

From this mass of preparatory documents, two papers had a profound effect upon the Chapter. One of them was from Mrs Louise Locke.

Louise had first come to Lee Abbey as a guest in 1949, when she was going through a very bleak time. She was suffering from bad health, her marriage was going wrong, and she had just moved into a house with ten rooms that was far too big for her. She had not been near a church for ages and did not care about religion at all. After a long talk with a member of the houseparty, she found herself standing up on the final evening to share with the other guests how she felt that 'a great load had gone from her shoulders'.

The following year she returned with her children,

and although she felt much happier, her health was still very poor. It was suggested that she might receive prayer with the laying on of hands and subsequently her health improved greatly.

She still had the problem of her over-large house. She had advertised for lodgers with no response until she received an unexpected telephone call. She described it thus:

> It was from Miss Hilda Porter, from the Methodist International House, asking me if I would take coloured students, as she said someone who wished to remain anonymous had told her that I not only wanted boarders, but that I would be the right person to look after these students. I said 'no' at first as I said I had never spoken to a coloured person and I was still afraid of people, but Miss Porter persuaded me to take my first girl. This was Pushpa, a very young Indian girl from Singapore who wanted to study Law. She was very charming. Pushpa said to me one day, 'I shall be twenty-one next week,' so I said that we had better have a tea party, and she said that she had no friends, but in the end asked if she could ask a lonely Nigerian student to tea – I said 'yes'. He was Igwe from Eastern Region. While he was with us he said it was nice to be inside a home, so I told him he could come again, and suggested that he came any Saturday for tea and bring a friend over. One Saturday I came home with the children from shopping and found seven Nigerians on the doorstep. I took them all in and gave them some tea and decided there and then to have tea parties on Sundays.

Thus began Louise's ministry to overseas students. It was not long before three bedrooms at her home in Tooting were constantly available as accommodation for students, and she would try to find accommodation for others through the local papers and the churches. She began monthly coffee evenings in her home which soon outgrew the house and had to be moved to a nearby hall. A newspaper reporter, fascinated by Louise's work, noted the carefully written notice on a bookcase in her sitting room: 'Unless everybody present understands your language – it's only common politeness to speak English!' She worked hard to bring the needs of overseas students to the attention of the churches of all denominations, and formed 'The Balham and Tooting International Circle'. The British Council heard about her and she began to work with them in local accommodation campaigns, and in sending out letters of welcome to some thousand overseas students each year. In response she received many requests for help and advice and sought to link up the students with churches.

Louise had close contacts with the Methodists and Roman Catholics and she greatly admired much that they were doing for students through their hostels; she longed to see her own Church of England showing a similar practical concern. So it was that when she received the request for ideas in preparation for the Chapter of Friends, Louise prepared a paper setting o ıt a scheme for a Lee Abbey Hostel in London for overseas students, which could also serve as a meeting place for Lee Abbey Friends.

Louise was not alone in her concern for overseas students. Another paper submitted to the Chapter on this subject came from Lt. Col. George Grimshaw, a former missionary who was working in the Overseas Visitors Department of CMS. In many ways his proposal was more ambitious than Louise's. He outlined his vision of a Christian Institute founded on an evangelical foundation with a residential nucleus of students and Community.

With a real sense of expectation, over 500 of the Lee

Abbey Friends finally assembled in a large marquee erected on the North Lawn for the Chapter, with its title 'Task for Tomorrow'. The tone for the whole week was set by Jack as he preached at the opening service in the packed Church of St Mary's, Lynton, reiterating the words of Francis 'What He has promised, let us fulfil – and to what we are promised, let us look forward'. Each day began with a Bible reading by Wallace Bird on 'The Kingdom of the Spirit', then sessions and discussion groups looked at the changing situations facing the nation and the Church. Each evening 'Meeting Point' provided a forum for everybody to listen to many of the ideas expressed in the preparatory papers being expounded.

Throughout the week the weather was generally very pleasant, but the wind blew as strongly as it can on the North Devon coast in the autumn. Indeed at times it looked as it if might lift the marquee off the ground. There were many Friends who were not slow to interpret this wind as a powerful sign from God of what He was wishing to do, not merely for Lee Abbey and the Friends, but for His whole Church.

As a result of the week a whole new area opened up for the mission of God through Lee Abbey. Few people can have gone away from the Chapter without the call to deeper commitment to Christ, His Church and the local community still ringing in their ears. Reports later evidenced this being worked out in practice. And at Lee Abbey itself, the team and the Council were left with a list of seven recommendations requiring discussions and action.

The next meeting of the Council began the enormous task of deciding how to implement these suggestions, but most of them were to flounder and come to nothing. One recommendation, however, that both the team and the Council felt compelled by God to pursue, was that involving overseas students. So a fact-finding committee, including Louise Locke and George Grimshaw and chaired by Gordon Mayo, was set up to look at the possibilities.

In close co-operation with Christian Team Work, the next year was spent in assessing the whole situation concerning overseas students resident in London, and the possible options open to Lee Abbey. There was plenty to encourage them. In 1961 the Government had announced that they were willing to make up to three million pounds available to voluntary bodies for capital expenditure on projects concerned with Commonwealth young people. Quite clearly the funds would be provided if a project was undertaken. This money was made available through OSWEP (Overseas Students Welfare Extension Programme) and was administered by the British Council. The grant was interest-free, did not need to be repaid, and would be written off over a period of twenty-five years. In addition, the London County Council was willing to offer mortgages for such projects at a fixed rate of interest, though this of course, did have to be repaid.

How different from the founding of Lee Abbey in Devon in 1945!

The committee also had the task of bringing together the two visions that had been outlined by George Grimshaw and Louise Locke at the Chapter, and the decision was taken that Lee Abbey should go ahead and establish a much larger hostel near the centre of London, run by a community, which would offer facilities as an International Centre.

So in 1963 the hunt was on to find suitable premises, before starting the complicated legal procedures necessary to obtain available grants. The committee, now chaired by Prebendary Denis Wakeling, was on the look-out for either a suitable site on which they could build a hostel, or existing property which they could adapt to their needs.

Then one day in the autumn two letters arrived at Lee Abbey. One was from a Friend who knew all about the hostel project. He had been walking through Courtfield Gardens, off the Earls Court Road in Kensington, and had seen 'For Sale' boards outside several adjacent hotels. The other letter, also from a Lee Abbey Friend, drew attention to the same hotels which were being advertised in the *Daily Telegraph*.

George Grimshaw was contacted and went to view the property. There were three separate hotels, Courtfield, Melbourne and Edinburgh, imposing Victorian buildings with white stucco fronts. They were within a short walking distance of each other and had been run as one establishment by the Overseas Visitors Club, an organisation providing accommodation mainly for white South Africans and Australians staying in London. As South Africa left the Commonwealth, so the club had gone out of business. The hotels were to be sold fully equipped down to the last detail, with the furnishings in Edinburgh virtually unused. The three properties were to be sold separately; they were almost ideal for what Lee Abbey had in mind.

As the day for the auction arrived, a vigil of prayer was arranged by the Community in the chapel. Frequent telephone calls were made between London and Devon as the day proceeded. However, it seemed at first as if God had suddenly said 'no' to the project, for one of the hotels, Melbourne, went to a higher bidder. However, following negotiations between the agents and the purchasers, eventually the three properties were obtained.

The next couple of months were to be ones of frantic activity. Lee Abbey had the property, which needed far less adaptation than anyone had imagined, so the work of accommodating students could begin almost as soon as the legal formalities had been completed. It had already been agreed that Gordon Mayo was the obvious person to be the first Warden of the Lee Abbey International Students Club, as it was to be called. The same Chapter meeting also agreed that three of the

Department leaders – Lily Dear, the secretary, Mary Hope, the head cook, and Chris Mail, the house leader – should go with Gordon and Sheila to form the nucleus of the London Community. The loss of so many key senior people at one time was to create a big gap in the Community of Devon, but once again these were pioneering days.

Because the legal work had still to be completed, it was as caretaker rather than Warden that Gordon with the other four, moved to London in January 1964. The first task for the London Community was to clean Courtfield, which housed the main kitchen, as it had been used as the restaurant for the club. The scene must have been very reminiscent of the early days in Devon as the Community, together with a very enthusiastic band of local Lee Abbey Friends, set about attacking layers of accumulated grease and dirt – a task made all the more difficult by the lack of any central heating or running hot water. A few days after they had arrived, George Grimshaw came to visit and brought some Forsythia from his garden. 'If this doesn't come out into bloom here, we'll know it's too cold for you!' Much to some people's amazement, it did.

It was decided that the Community and students would live together in the three houses. The planned accommodation was for 180 students: 100 from Commonwealth countries, 30 from other countries, with the rest from Britain. The British Council were only too delighted to be able to direct recently arrived students to a new hostel.

The buildings had cost £236,000. The combined OSWEP grant and the LCC mortgage meant that only £6,000 had to be found by Lee Abbey itself. However, these grants were made on the security of the deeds of the Lee Abbey estate, and immediately an appeal was launched to the Lee Abbey Friends so that the deeds might be released as quickly as possible.

Lee Abbey in London

It would be hard to imagine two more contrasting places than Lynton and Earls Court, but both were now to be home for the two parts of the Lee Abbey Community. Here was to be the great test for the Community life that had evolved over the last nineteen years, as the London Community sought to express a corporate life in this urban multi-racial setting. It was not easy.

Just over a month after Melbourne House had started to receive students Sheila wrote, with real excitement, to the Community back in Devon.

We have over twenty nationalities now and the comments and reactions are very interesting. Our Yugoslavian doctor who has done a doctorate in languages (Persian included) but whose English is rather less than perfect told Pauline the other night that he admired her structure! He stands at the counter in the kitchen and says in a pathetic voice, 'How to be happy? You are happy. Why?' Margaret Njoke, our Kikuyu member told him of Jesus which to him meant *nothing*. Jesus? Who is that? Meanwhile we try to live the sort of life which speaks louder than sermons. Our charming Muslim (one of many) Yusufu Mohammed, from Northern Nigeria, asked to take his shoes off in the chapel and I think considered us as second-class religious because we only pray three times a day!

They soon discovered that there was no shortage of students seeking accommodation. The temptation was to take too many before there were enough Community members to staff the place. As the Community grew in numbers so Courtfield came into use and finally Edinburgh, so that by the autumn the International Students Club had reached its full capacity of 180 students from thirty-nine different countries and six different religions, about two-thirds being Christians.

111

The small Community of twenty-one members had
much to learn. For instruction in the actual mechan-
ics of running the place, a great deal of help was
received from the established overseas student hostels like William Temple House and the Methodist
International House. For their Community life they
adopted the same pattern of structure and worship
as in Devon, with probationary and full members,
Community prayers each morning, Community intercessions and the weekly corporate Communion. In
place of red and green labels, which it was thought
would be totally out of place in a residential hostel,
they had a distinctive lapel badge. It was an ancient
Egyptian symbol discovered by Gordon and Sheila,
a small anchor cross. As the main dining room in
Courtfield had many nautical trappings and was called
the Compass Room, it seemed a natural symbol for the
Community to adopt.

Part of one of John Donne's poems ('To Mr George
Herbert, with one of my seals, of the anchor and
Christ') emphasises the significance of the anchor
cross:

> The Crosse (my seal at Baptism) spread below,
> Does, by that form, into an Anchor grow.
> Crosses grow Anchors; Bear, as thou shouldst do
> Thy Crosse, an that Crosse grows an Anchor too.
> But he that makes our Crosses Anchors thus,
> Is Christ, who there is crucified for us.

Although much of the basic structure of Community life
could be transferred to London, it soon became apparent that their task was very different. The assumption
had always been that the London Community would
relate to the students in much the same way as the
Devon Community did to the guests: this was not so.
In Devon the house is home for the Community; the
guests come for their brief stay and then leave. At

oger de Pemberton greets the Bishop of Exeter

edication Day, June 1946

Haymaking, early fifties

Ursula Kay in the old farm (*right*)

General view in the fifties (*below*)

Jack Winslow leading a walk, clergy recess 1950

the fifties: Back row (left to right): Jack Winslow, Geoffrey Rogers, ?, Leslie Sutton;
front row, second from left: Madeline Wheen.

The chapel 1995 (*above*)

Geoffrey Paul
installed
as Warden
1970. (*right*)

The Pastoral Team, 1985; far left John and Gay Perry.

Compass Room
he sixties (*above*)

The Lee Abbey International Students Club
Courtfield House (*right*)

ving, September 1982

The Suncourt Hotel, the current Club

A celebration buffet.

Dedication: (from left to right):
Denis Wakeling, Lord Belstead,
Mike and Sue Battison.

51 Lincoln Road, Walsall (*above*)

Lee Abbey Three: Aston, 121 Albert Road (*left*)

(In the centre) Audrey Martin Doyle

Communion on
the beach (*above*)

The Tea Cottage

The Youth Camp, 1981

the Club the students are the residents, many staying up to three years, much longer than the majority of Community members. In Devon the relationship was that of hosts to guests; in London it was management to residents. It was essential that the students, who were not necessarily Christians, should be consulted and involved in the running of the Club.

The Community were not merely endeavouring to express the life of Lee Abbey in London; what was more important was for them to work out its mission. Initially there were those, including some Council members, who assumed that the London Club would be like Lynton with regular teaching sessions and evening 'evangelistic epilogues'. Unease had been expressed when it was learned that the British Council grant was dependent upon an undertaking that there could be no proselytising. Clarification revealed that this referred to compulsion for people to change their religion, which was not what Lee Abbey understood by evangelism! Through staying at the Club some students became Christians, testifying to their new-found faith through baptism and confirmation. This brought deep joy to the Community, but it was not the primary purpose of the Club. Evangelism was seen much more in terms of being a Christian presence, rather than simply making converts; leading the kind of life and saying the kind of things that allowed the Good News of Christ to become evident.

The Community came to realise that God was calling them to witness in three major areas; their work, their life and worship, and their words. The first was in the provision of good-quality hostel accommodation. This was easier said than done. At the very first resident's meeting, the obvious forum for student complaints, Gordon was earnestly promising everyone that all the small repairs that needed doing would be attended to as quickly as possible, when a flood from a bathroom on the fourth floor began to pour down! Erratic plumbing and the antiquated central heating system caused a steady stream of complaints. A more serious problem was a major outbreak of dry rot in both Courtfield and Edinburgh, which not only disrupted life for everybody for months with the noise and upheaval of builders, but also placed a heavy financial burden on the Club, which had little surplus money.

It also proved a perplexing form of witness for the students. Many of them came from countries where it was impossible to conceive of the people in authority as also being the servants. It was hard to grasp that the people who ran and, as they assumed, owned the place, were also those who did the basic domestic work; cleaning lavatories, answering the telephone or cooking the meals. Here was one of the revolutionary features of the Christian faith – Jesus came to serve, not to be served.

The Community were not only providing a place to live, but also a home. Some students would come and stay at the Club for a few months after first arriving in Britain and then move on once they had found a flat or other accommodation. Others would stay for several years. For many it could be lonely and bewildering living in London, a society which had little time for students and especially for those from overseas, who were often made to feel that they were parasites, living off another country. They needed a place where they could feel accepted, whatever their race or religion, where they would find friendship and could be themselves.

The Community's life and worship together was another important tool in witnessing to the students. Even if they did not realise it before they arrived, no student was left in any doubt that it was a group of Christians who ran Lee Abbey.

A real affinity was experienced between those who were believers. The great divide was not so much between the Christians and the rest, as between those

who were people of faith, be it Christian, Hindu or
Muslim, and those who had abandoned their original
belief in their attempts to assert their identity or
break away from their past. In the face of atheistic
opposition, perhaps from a Marxist, the Christian and
Muslim would find themselves standing together. As
anywhere, sorrow and joy drew people together. A
young Jamaican law student died under anaesthetic
when in hospital for a minor operation, and that evening half the Club packed into the chapel to mourn and
listen to the Scriptures. On another occasion different
religions were drawn together in worship to share the
joy of a couple who were married in the chapel.

Although anybody was welcome to join the Community at prayers, it was always made clear that this was
Christian worship. At the second Christmas, when the
Community were observing the midnight service as
their corporate Communion, the evangelistic power
of the Eucharist was demonstrated in a remarkable
way. It was held in the Compass Room with an open
invitation to the students. It was clearly explained that
this was the celebration of the birth of Christ and to
most people's surprise a large group of Israelis, some
Hindus and a number of orthodox Muslims came to
the service. However, they had not come merely to
spectate. When the Christians came forward to receive
the Sacrament, they came forward with them. For
the Community it was a deeply moving experience,
especially when afterwards several of them commented
that it was the first time in their lives that they had
experienced the presence of God. But a community does
not only witness when it is worshipping. 'If you have
love for one another than everyone will know that you
are my disciples,' Jesus told His disciples. They were
very much 'on show' the whole time and the students
were only too conscious of everything that went on.
They saw a group of people seeking to love and care
for each other, working out the Christian values of

love, justice and forgiveness in everyday life. They were equally aware when things were not right, and would note how the Community coped with personality clashes, grudges and petty jealousies.

The third area of witness was the witness of the spoken word. 'Why are you here?' 'Why work for so little money?' students might ask. Some would be curious, others mildly mocking. There was rarely an epilogue to verbalise the Gospel; it was up to the Community members to give a reason for 'the hope that was within them'. If they wanted to share what they believed, then they quickly learned that they had to be prepared to listen and learn from others before they could expect a hearing. It was not easy for a young Community member, often with no knowledge of other religions, to find himself in debate perhaps with a student studying for a Ph.D. who was intellectually superior and determined to argue.

As the mission of the Club began to be worked out in practice, it became clear that Christians of considerable spiritual maturity would be required if this work were to be done properly. At almost every meeting of the Council the Warden's reports referred to the difficulty in finding Community members who were prepared to stay for a couple of years. This problem was not peculiar to the Club. In Devon Madeleine was finding similar difficulty in recruiting suitable girls, and in the wider Church, numbers offering for ordination were down, as were applications to the missionary societies. It was a feature of the sixties. In Gordon and Sheila, together with several other long-term members, the Community enjoyed strong leadership, but the continually changing membership and the shortage of staff was a constant strain. The Lee Abbey Community was not a place for those who were seeking a secure role; the relationship between Community and students could not be easily defined.

By the time Chris Hayward succeeded Gordon as

Warden in 1971, the Club was increasingly reflecting
the full diversity of the student world. Initially it
was assumed that the majority of the students would
be doing postgraduate and undergraduate courses at
the colleges in West London, and especially Imperial
College, which is close to Earls Court. As time went on
an incredible variety of students were staying at the
Club. 'From forty different countries, doing forty different courses, at forty different colleges,' was the reply
normally given to those enquiring about the sort of
students who lived at the Lee Abbey Club. The courses
ranged from hairdressing to hotel management, from
architecture to aeronautical engineering; there were
those doing postgraduate research, and those spending
a year in London learning basic English at a private
language school.

As the students completed their courses and returned
home so the true significance of the ministry of the Lee
Abbey Club became apparent. Many were the intellectual elite of their society and returned to positions of
great responsibility and influence. Some of those who
had lived at the Club became Government ministers,
or took up senior posts in the legal and medical
professions, the Civil Service and industry. The vast
majority had not made any commitment to Christ,
and had possibly not even expressed any interest
in the Christian faith – the Club had merely been
a convenient place to stay – but for two years they
had been with a Christian community, witnessing their
life and the presence of the Holy Spirit whose work
is not limited to the Church. There is no knowing
what seeds were sown or what fruit will emerge in
the years ahead.

The work of Lee Abbey in London was clearly established, but it was not easy to relate it to the work in
Devon. When it was set up many people had assumed
that it would be similar to Scargill in its relationship
to the Devon Community, but the Council decided that

they should be seen as one Community operating in two different ways. Devon and London were 'two expressions of the same concept' with the same basis of membership but independent in organisation.

There were natural links between them. Each found real encouragement in knowing that every morning Community members were praying for each other using the monthly prayer diary. Exchanges were arranged so that members of different departments experienced each other's work at first hand. It was good for the Club to be able to take groups of students down to Devon to see Lee Abbey and to enjoy the Devon countryside. For some people, this relationship was more than just a means of mutual encouragement; the existence of the London part of the Community was evidence of Lee Abbey working out its original vision more fully. The two parts needed each other. The Club needed the experience, financial backing and reputation of the Devon establishment, while Lee Abbey, which was sometimes accused of being too comfortable and isolated, could point to the work in London as evidence of its 'front-line' involvement.

It was not easy for either Community to feel the closeness of the bond that they had in theory. One difficulty was that they did not know each other. At the beginning, all the London Community had served in Devon. However, as new members joined, many of them never having visited Devon, it became increasingly difficult at both ends for people to put faces to the names on the prayer list. The joint Chapter meetings and the exchanges helped them to get to know each other but with a continual turnover of members this was far from easy. Initially the London Community had adopted the pattern of life developed in Devon, but this was altered to fit their ministry so that after a while the two groups were using different Community promises, a different scale of allowances, and a different organisational structure. It was a natural development that caused them to be regarded as two separate communities.

During one of the very first visits of a party from the Club to Devon, Madeleine was sitting next to one of the students at dinner. By way of conversation she asked him, 'Where do you come from?'

'Oh, I come from Lee Abbey,' he replied. 'Have you ever been there?'

It was very clear that the Lee Abbey Fellowship now embraced not one, but two very important and very different works of God.

Chapter 8
'A New Work of the Spirit'

'I am asking for an openness to new ideas, a willingness to experiment which will not stifle the Holy Spirit if, as I believe He does, He wishes to do new things in new ways in a new age.'

Donald Coggan was preaching the sermon at the 1964 Reunion Service in St Paul's Cathedral. Few people could have realised how prophetic his words were, as he continued, 'This means that, if we give the Holy Spirit a chance, He will make Jesus so real to us that we shall see Him not as a figure of ancient history, but as our great Contemporary; and the results are not likely to be less disturbing than they were nineteen centuries back.'

Disturbing was the right word to describe the impact on the Church of the work of God, which was to bring renewed prominence to the person and work of the Holy Spirit. As books like *The Cross and the Switchblade* and *They Speak with Other Tongues* became popular, so the charismatic movement was the great subject of discussion at Christian gatherings, with those passionately in favour, those definitely against and many who were genuinely questioning and seeking. In its response to the charismatic movement Lee Abbey was to mirror what was happening in the wider Church.

The first recognition of the impact of the movement on Lee Abbey was recorded by Geoffrey Rogers in his final report to the Council as Warden in October 1964. After noting that the power of the Holy Spirit had been increasingly at work during the summer season he wrote, 'The particular manifestation of private glossolalia has appeared, sought and unsought among members of the Community and more than a dozen members (almost, but not entirely all women members) are now speaking in tongues in their own private devotions'.

Geoffrey's initial reaction to the emergence of a group within the Community who were speaking in tongues was one of caution. He had only recently heard news from a parish, with which Lee Abbey had had close links over many years, of a deep split in the congregation over this issue; it was one of the first Anglican parishes in England to experience this new movement of the Holy Spirit. Some bad mistakes had been made in the initial enthusiasm. Geoffrey was most anxious that no similar division should be allowed to arise within the Community and so weaken its evangelistic impact. He also realised that Lee Abbey was in a position of considerable influence in the Church of England, and many people would be looking to the Community for guidance and would take a lead from their response.

A guarded editorial on the subject was published in *Christian Witness*. It welcomed the reappearance of speaking in tongues within the Church and recognised that 'It can be a means of wonderful spiritual uplift and blessing to the receiver, and often a new beginning of Spirit-led life and experience,' but followed this with a clear warning.

What those who have received the gift need to guard against is the spiritual pride which supposes that because of it they are higher in God's favour than those who have not received it, or that they alone have received the Baptism of the Holy Spirit and are Christians in the full sense. It is this attitude that can easily cause and has at times caused divisions among the brethren and the destruction of Christian fellowship.

It was not long before there were several of the Community who had had some kind of charismatic experience, which usually involved speaking in tongues. Some of them felt that the leaders did not share their enthusiasm and were being over-cautious in their approach. Geoffrey ruled that there should be no exclusive meetings for the exercise of the spiritual gifts and chapters twelve to fourteen of 1 Corinthians were used at the Community prayers to study the use and abuse of spiritual gifts. A similar approach was taken by Ken Pillar when he became Warden; there was to be no use of tongues in public, although private meetings could be held provided that they were open to any who wished to come.

There was no official Lee Abbey policy on the movement, because no such policy was possible. The Community, and especially the Chapter, contained those to whom their 'Baptism in the Spirit' experience had revolutionised their Christian lives, those who could testify to such an experience in the past but for whom it was less significant, and those who could claim no such experience. The challenge that the charismatic movement presented to Lee Abbey was whether such a mixed group could openly live, work and pray together, fully accepting one another in Christ and recognising that each had a continual need of the Spirit's touch. At the time of writing (spring, 1995) the 'Toronto Blessing' is raising again very similar issues for the Community. As Lee Abbey had always insisted on the necessity for personal conversion, so it had always claimed the necessity for Christians to be continually open to and filled by the Holy Spirit. In this work God was not limited to certain experiences or ways of working. The leaders of the Community believed that Lee Abbey needed to include those who came with different experiences of God and so of the Holy Spirit.

As with the issue of churchmanship, Lee Abbey appeared enigmatic concerning the charismatic movement. Guests would not hear talks from Community members about Baptism in the Spirit or seeking spiritual gifts, but Michael and Jeanne Harper were invited as guest speakers. Although guests were not told that they ought to be seeking a charismatic experience, those who came to Lee Abbey conscious of their need of something new would often find God leading them to a Community member or a fellow guest who would talk and pray with them.

Such was the case at the Families Houseparty in June 1963. A number of young couples who were hungry for more of the Holy Spirit in their lives met together with two of the chaplains. Not really knowing what to do, they all prayed for each other in turn with laying on of hands, open to the Lord for whatever He might want to do. As they met to pray it marked the start of a new experience of the Holy Spirit 'sweeping through them'. John and Gay Perry were among the group and their ministry in Chorleywood was transformed as a result of that time. Indeed, God was preparing them to return eventually to Lee Abbey when John was appointed Warden some thirteen years later. A number of senior Community members who had received a spiritual gift would exercise it freely in their ministry; for example, quietly praying in tongues during a service of prayer with the laying on of hands. However, many guests from churches which had experienced a great movement of the Spirit were anxious that Lee Abbey should take a much more positive line in encouraging every Christian to seek a second blessing experience and to speak in tongues.

As it became increasingly obvious that this was not merely a nine-day wonder but a new spiritual movement throughout the world-wide Church, the true significance of what God was doing became clear. The fundamental issue was not about spiritual experience but about renewal. The work of God is to renew continually the lives of individuals – a constant process of which conversion is but the beginning – and to renew the Church as the people of God, leading in turn to the renewal of society. The Holy Spirit was reminding the Church of truths that had largely been forgotten, in practice if not in theory. It became obvious that many of the truths the charismatic movement was propounding were those Lee Abbey had been seeking to demonstrate since 1945.

Teaching on the use and place of spiritual gifts in building up the Body of Christ, on healing, on lay ministry and on freedom in worship, did not seem as revolutionary at Lee Abbey as it did in many other places. The Community was a body of Christ's people in which many of these things were already being worked out and it was ripe for new encouragement. The ministry of healing was one such area.

For many years this had been part of Lee Abbey's ministry, mainly under the guidance of Jack Winslow. It was perfectly normal to pray for those who were sick, together with the laying on of hands and sometimes with anointing with oil. There was a real expectation that results would be seen and there were many people who could testify to experiencing God's healing touch.

As a result of the renewed interest in the ministry of healing, an American, Agnes Sanford, well-known through her books, such as *The Healing Light*, was invited as a guest speaker on several occasions, including a number of clergy recesses. With her teaching on the healing of the memories, she brought a whole new dimension to the subject. She laid stress on the work of the Holy Spirit, informally introducing a number of people for the first time to the idea of 'Baptism in the Holy Spirit'. As well as her public speaking

she counselled and prayed with a number of people
for healing and both guests and Community members were blessed through her ministry. Throughout
she stressed the need to bring healing back into the
centre of the Church's life and worship. Many of the
clergy returned to establish a healing ministry in their
parishes and for the Community a consequence of her
visit was that renewed prominence was given to prayer
with the laying on of hands at the corporate Communion. There would be very few weeks at Lee Abbey in
which there was not a service of prayer for healing. But
although Agnes's visit brought a renewed confidence in
the power of God to heal, the Community also had to
discover the much harder lesson that physical recovery
is not automatically the will of God. There was one
person for whom Agnes said that she felt it was not
right to pray for recovery, and whom God used to teach
the Community most about His power to heal.

Lily Lloyd was a great character in the Community. She came from a humble home in Cambridge,
where she had been converted at Holy Trinity Church.
Though she had few educational advantages, she had
a natural wit and intelligence and could confound the
wisest academics with her simple and direct faith.
She came to Lee Abbey as second cook and her lively
sense of humour and fund of entertaining stories about
her experiences in the ATS 'on the gun site' made
the kitchen a place of much laughter. Being short
of stature she was provided with a stool on which
to stand when stirring the various mixtures brewing
on the big ranges of the old kitchen. There she would
stand and hold forth, her ringing voice and laughter
carrying up through the yard to the chapel windows.
She was never afraid to speak out if she saw anything
wrong, but she had a warm and loving personality.
Sadly, however, she developed cancer and had to have
a mastectomy. Her return to Community life coincided
with the purchase of Lee Mouth Cottage.

The owner, Mrs Budd, whose father had been woodsman for Squire Bailey, had decided that she ought to give up her cottage and move into Lynton. As the cottage was situated in the middle of the estate, next to the camp field and the road to the beach, Lee Abbey was most anxious to buy it and Mrs Budd was quite happy to sell.

It seemed ideal, once the cottage had been modernised, that Lil should live there together with her friend Ursula, who ran the farm. She could continue the Devon cream tea business for which Mrs Budd had established quite a reputation in the area. But within two years the cancer had reappeared and Lil was very ill. Groups of the Community would gather round her bed to pray with her; there was real confidence that God would want to heal Lil and restore her to full health. It seemed natural when Agnes Sanford next visited to ask her to pray for Lil, and a real improvement was expected. Agnes taught, however, that before one prayed for healing it was essential to pray for guidance about God's will for the person, and she replied that she did not believe that it was God's will for her to pray for Lil's physical healing. It was hard to accept and understand. A couple of weeks later another guest, with wide experience in the healing ministry, was asked if she would pray for Lil. She laid hands on her claiming Christ's healing power, but Lil's physical decline continued and six months later she died.

Lil's illness and death were to have a profound effect upon the Community, bringing new depths of understanding about the power of the Holy Spirit and the ways of God. If there was a guest who seemed very preoccupied with their own problems it was often suggested that they might go down to the cottage to cheer up Lil. They would return astonished at her serenity and testimony to the love of God. God had given Lil the very special gift of being able to speak about her faith without any embarrassment.

The beautiful garden at the cottage which was created by landscaping a corner of the neighbouring field now stands as a permanent memorial to Lil. It is a picture of the work of God, the Holy Spirit, who transforms ordinary, rough lives to bring beauty, joy and peace.

* * *

In the middle of the turmoil and excitement that characterised the sixties Lee Abbey celebrated the twenty-first anniversary of the establishment of the work in Devon with a great gathering in London. Cuthbert Bardsley reiterated the convictions on which Lee Abbey was founded as he preached at a Eucharist at St Martin-in-the-Fields.

> This could be a dangerous moment, if we were merely to rest content with the point that we have reached. What is God saying to us of Lee Abbey today? I believe that God is saying first, that nothing less than a major reformation is needed in Britain today, and second, if that is to happen, the Church must get her priorities right; evangelism must be restored to its rightful place in the scale of the Church's values. And third, if that is to happen, we must be far more deeply converted than most of us are at this moment. And fourth, if that is to happen we must be brought once again, face to face with a living, loving, saving Lord – the Lord of Calvary.'

In the afternoon the strength of the Lee Abbey movement was demonstrated when over 6,000 people filled the Royal Albert Hall for the rally, which included a testimony and two songs from Cliff Richard, whose recent conversion was still headline news. The theme was 'Time to Build ... Time to Serve ... Time to Act', and Donald Coggan, now Archbishop of York, threw down the challenge of Christian service to young people.

It was not only changes in the presentation of the Gospel and in theological thinking that guests at Lee Abbey began to notice during the sixties. The place was becoming more comfortable. This was a decade of affluence. Harold Macmillan had told the country that 'they had never had it so good', and materially he was right. The generally improved standard of living meant that guests could no longer be expected to put up with the relatively spartan conditions of the early years. If Lee Abbey were to attract holiday visitors, then it must offer the standard of accommodation and service found in private hotels. No longer were guests asked to bring their own sheets, and the purchase of a dishwasher meant that it was possible to dispense with the need for guests to take their turn at the sinks. These improvements were a mixed blessing, for although it greatly added to the comfort of a holiday at Lee Abbey, guests and Community were no longer working together as before. A clearer distinction was emerging which saw the Community as those who served, and the guests as those who were being served.

Holiday visitors were also becoming accustomed to higher standards of accommodation. People were less willing to share rooms and Lee Abbey having only two single bedrooms, it was decided to mark the anniversary by building a block of twelve new single rooms.

While the builders were at work on this new bedroom block the Community maintenance team were tackling the largest job they had ever faced – the rewiring of virtually the whole house in preparation for the changeover from generating their own electricity to the mains supply.

As the improvements in facilities were making life more comfortable for the guests, for the Community they presented a new dilemma. Community membership no longer involved the material and physical sacrifice of the early days. Allowances were not large but with full board and keep provided, Lee Abbey offered a very secure job. There was no longer any question that there would not be sufficient money at the end of the week for allowances to be paid. Accommodation was cramped, but central heating meant that for many they were far warmer than they would have been at home. Machines like floor polishers and dishwashers meant that much of the work was no longer so hard. A number of people felt that there was a danger that community life could become a soft option rather than the challenge that it had been before. Real disquiet was expressed at the news that the corridors were going to be carpeted. This decision was seen as symbolic that the pioneering days were over; the house would be much quieter and easier to clean, but for many, Lee Abbey was becoming more like a hotel than the home of a Christian community.

Yet, as life was getting easier, Community members were also given greater responsibility. Whatever their task they have always been expected to befriend guests and be prepared to be used by God to listen and to witness. Departmental duties meant that in practice this contact with the guests was restricted to mealtimes and evenings. The general responsibility for the houseparty programme and pastoral work lay with the chaplains and other senior members and about half a dozen of the guests, who each week were invited to join the houseparty team.

Changes began to be made which enabled much greater involvement of the whole Community in the direct ministry to guests. At first it was decided that one red-label member from each department should be chosen each week to join the houseparty team, to attend the morning team meeting and report back to his department on matters that needed specific prayer. It was then seen that as part of their training it would be good to involve Community members in planning programmes, attending sessions, leading walks and various activities.

These changes enabled a structure to develop which

recognised that pastoral work belonged to the whole Community and allowed gifts to be discovered and more fully used. This involvement has continued to increase steadily so that Community members are now released full-time from departmental duties throughout their week on the team, to share in all the guests' activities.

During the sixties Lee Abbey seemed to be walking through a minefield. Advance meant that risks had to be taken; wrong moves were made and explosions were set off. Yet the Community was very much alive, if a bit battered as it entered the seventies.

Chapter 9
Under Canvas

'I can't stand it here!' moaned a young girl. 'I've never been surrounded by so much love, I want to go home.'

It was 5.00 p.m. on a Saturday afternoon. An hour before she had arrived at the Lee Abbey Youth Camp, been given a name badge, allocated to a tent and handed a plastic mug of rather indifferent tea! Not a word had been spoken to her about the Christian faith, but she could sense that the place was totally foreign to her experience. Later she was grateful that she had been persuaded to stay.

Each August the field below the house overlooking the bay is the setting for the summer camps. On this truly sacred ground many have met with the living God and had all their adult life changed as a result.

Crockpits – the headland beyond Lee Bay – was the site of a small camp in 1947, but the first camp organised on the present field was in 1948. Far less exposed, it has proved ideal: it slopes down towards the sea, drains quickly and is protected from the prevailing south-westerly wind by the hillside. Only when the wind is from the north-west, a fairly rare event, does everybody have to be prepared to hold down the tents!

The first Commandant, as the leader of the camp used to be styled, was Arthur Westall, a teacher who had become a Christian at Lee Abbey the previous summer. He and his wife had been wondering where to go on holiday when she noticed an advertisement for Lee Abbey in a newspaper used to wrap up some fish.

'Here is the place for us, nice and cheap and grand country.' He looked at it.

'Not for me,' he said. 'Church of England Centre! They will want to shove religion down our throats there.' But his wife got her way, and they came. Although he was the headmaster of a Church School, and a church warden, he had lost his Christian faith. During the holiday the friendliness he encountered melted his suspicions. The absence of 'buttonholing' put him at ease and he became intrigued by the spirit of the place. The fresh presentation of the old truth brought a return of faith and he sought out one of the speakers and with his help renewed his commitment to Christ. He went back to his work with a new vision and new zest, and his staff and pupils alike were conscious of the change. The next year God used Arthur's new-found faith as a powerful instrument in establishing the Youth Camp.

For the first two years the camp was distinctly makeshift in its organisation. There were virtually no special facilities on the field itself other than the large marquee used for eating and meetings, and the latrines. Nearby streams were used for washing, the cooks alone being allowed the privilege of going up to the main house for baths. Bell tents were hired from the Army. For both cooking and hot water they relied on a couple of open-air field kitchens, which were very difficult to use, especially in the rain.

This was all changed when Raymond Scantlebury, always referred to as 'Scant' took over as Commandant in 1950. Under his leadership the whole thing was put on a much more organised footing, with ridge tents for sleeping and a fire shelter to ease the cooks' task.

Scant's influence on the camp was enormous. Infectious in his faith in Christ, he was a gifted evangelist. He had wanted to go to Africa as a missionary with

CMS but he was not physically strong and therefore not permitted to go overseas. Instead he was appointed as Canon Missioner in Carlisle Diocese, a post which offered plenty of scope for him to fulfil his calling to preach the Gospel.

Two particular qualities characterised his ministry. As a non-academic he could convey simple truths to intellectual people, and he possessed that rare gift of friendliness that was able to convince everyone to whom he spoke that he really cared about them and loved them. But above all he encouraged high expectations of God. It was the charismatic approach in the days before the charismatic movement. He believed that God was going to work miracles and people were going to be converted and that was why God had brought them to the camp. Each year saw his faith vindicated.

This was not high-pressure evangelism; indeed his approach was the exact opposite. A camper who wished to talk to Scant had to seek him out and he would not make it easy. As often as not someone asking to talk about a problem would be met with, 'Now I shall be busy for the next twenty minutes, would you do something for me, just go over to the chapel tent and put your problem to Jesus, just talk to Him about it. In about half an hour I shall be free.' Some time later that day Scant would search the person out.

'By the way, you wanted to come and see me.'

'Oh, well, I don't need to now because while I was in the chapel tent . . .'

It was an approach which demonstrated that his confidence was in God and not in himself.

Scant's death in 1958, only a few months before he was to lead the camp for his ninth successive year, was a great loss to Lee Abbey. The mantle of leadership passed to Reg Sanger who had been Scant's adjutant and he did the job for the next two years.

With two outside houseparties as well as a full

house, August was the busiest time of the year for the Community. For this reason the camp has always been organised separately from the work of the main house. For the next few years, however, leadership was taken over by the chaplains. The question of the leadership became a matter for much prayer, until one afternoon Ray Fardon, a member of the camp team for many years under Scant, came over to visit Lee Abbey from an outside houseparty being organised by Lee Abbey at St Audries. He talked with one of the chaplains and the result was that a few days later he received an invitation to take over the leadership of the camp. Although accepting 'for a year until one of the chaplains is free to take it on again', he was to be the Commandant for the next twelve years.

Ray closely followed the approach that Scant had established. He held the deep conviction that every single person was brought to camp by God with a definite purpose. The team were to pray that God would not allow anyone to come whom He was not going to bless and Ray would encourage them to look for nothing less than one hundred per cent conversions from camps even when at times only one in ten of those coming were Christians. To the outsider this approach might seem naive and arrogant yet it was taken afresh each year, in the belief that camp was a very special work of God and that this was what God was challenging them to ask of Him.

Each year would see their prayers answered, and if they did not see every camper confessing faith in Christ during the fortnight, there was real thanksgiving in the knowledge that God was touching, in different ways, the lives of all who had been present.

On Ray's retirement in 1978, the camp leadership was again taken over by one of the chaplains, Mike Battison. He had long associations with the camp, having been both a camper and then a regular team member. Even though he moved to London to become

Warden of the Lee Abbey International Students' Club
in 1983 he remained as camp leader until 1986, continuing very much in the tradition of Ray and Scant.

During a period of much experimentation and questioning of evangelistic strategy in the Church, and
even at Lee Abbey, at camp the basic approach did
not alter. Nor was any change needed. Each year it
was evident that God was powerfully blessing the
ministry. It was generally felt that a number of factors
contributed to this.

Firstly, there was the strong clear leadership. Secondly, there was the team. As Lee Abbey's ministry
is that of the Community led by the Warden, so the
camp's is that of the team led by the Commandant.
The team came to have a far more significant role
than merely undertaking all the practical jobs. At
the early camps it was a very haphazard process that
brought the team together. There was usually a group
of students from the London College of Divinity, but
otherwise it was a matter of friends inviting friends.
As everything became more organised under Scant so
people were selected in advance and a preparatory
weekend was introduced. It was held around Easter
and enabled the team to get to know each other, to do
advance planning and pray together.

Although the team was only together for a maximum
of five weeks each year – two fortnight camps with a
setting-up week before – a close fellowship developed.
One reason was that the majority of members, who
may previously have been campers, stayed on the team
for three or four years and so in any year at least
two-thirds would have served together before. Other
informal meetings such as reunions and weddings
maintained links through the year.

This bond within the team continues to be the foundation of the camp's Christian witness. Each tent is
led by a team member whose responsibility is both the
practical and spiritual welfare of those campers. At the

heart of camp is the daily team meeting which can last for anything up to two hours before lunch! Here they worship together, plan the next day's programme and pray in depth for each member of the camp. Experience has taught that until the team is truly united then spiritual progress on camp is slow.

It has always been felt that the age group of sixteen to twenty-five was significant. By maintaining a minimum age of sixteen, other than the children of team members, the camp had a very different ethos than most young people's camps, which would tend to be dominated by younger people.

Shifting social patterns mean that there have been changes over the years among those who come as campers. Initially the camp was advertised for sixteen- to thirty-year-olds, but the upper limit was soon lowered to twenty-five. In the fifties it was usually a very mature group with the average age over twenty. With the ending of National Service, the camp became younger, the majority being teenagers. Later another major change was noticed: after many years of camps where most were non-Christians, it was clear that now many of those coming had already made some form of commitment to Christ. This was a consequence of the general spiritual awakening taking place among young people, often through the renewal movement.

A surprising feature of camp, given its spiritual impact, has always been the lack of organised meetings and activities. For many years the only meetings were a voluntary Bible study before breakfast and the evening epilogue. With an increasing number of Christian campers, it was felt that there was a need to provide more teaching and so there was a slight expansion of the programme at the beginning of the eighties, when a morning teaching session was introduced – a time of worship replacing the pre-breakfast Bible Study. The programme, however, was still very unstructured compared with similar Christian camps, with campers largely free to do exactly as they wished, swim, laze in the sun, go on walks or have a cream tea at the cottage over the fence.

The focus of the ministry was and continues to be, the evening epilogue. This is the one time the whole camp is expected to be together. Although this is not compulsory there is strong encouragement to attend. One of the few camp rules is that everybody must be present on the field by 9.00 p.m. – when the epilogue begins.

During the sixties, while epilogues in the house were tending to get shorter, at camp they began to get longer and seldom lasting less than an hour, they were made up of worship and teaching. The well-established logical pattern which looked in turn at God, Man, Sin, Jesus, the Holy Spirit and the Christian life, continued to be followed even when it was no longer being used at the house. In content the epilogues have always attempted to reflect the swiftly changing needs of young people in each generation. In the sixties the challenge of the so-called 'new morality' and the questioning of biblical truth and authority meant that a strong emphasis was placed on the importance and integrity of the Bible as God's unchanging Word.

In the mid-seventies the massive general interest in the occult became a dominating issue. In personal counselling many campers required help and ministry because of their dabbling with ouija boards, spiritism and other occult practices, which at the time had appeared harmless but which resulted in a spiritual bondage. This necessitated careful teaching about spiritual warfare.

Towards the end of the seventies and into the eighties, the frequent breakdown of relationships within the family was becoming a decisive influence in the experience of young people. The 'Personal Relationships' epilogue had always been of crucial importance, coming at the end of the first week of camp before the challenge evening. Now, with many campers coming from broken and divided homes, nearly all the opening epilogues were built around this subject, with emphasis on Christ's work in reconciliation, the need to forgive and accept forgiveness, and the power of the Holy Spirit to change lives and situations. This approach to the Gospel has been found to communicate to many young people and bring healing to their own family situations.

The rest of the programme has seen surprisingly few alterations and several events have become established traditions. For example, every year visitors to the estate witness the spectacle of the entire camp in fancy dress, marching up the toll road to challenge the houseparty to the game of Podex or Crocker. Facing the common enemy is invaluable in uniting the camp, although victory is not a foregone conclusion! Camp sports are always included in the programme although there is now less emphasis on physical activity.

The pattern, established by Scant, was maintained for almost forty years. During the eighties, however, there were to be a number of major changes. In 1986 when Mike Battison retired as leader, for the first time the leadership of the two camps was split with Chris and Pat Rogers leading the first camp and Dave and Judy Gait the second camp. While a number of the team continued to come for five weeks there was no longer to be the sense of continuity of the previous years. There was to be a significant improvement of the facilities, which, while very well-organised, had seen few concessions to modern amenities with open fires still being used for cooking and cold water for showers. The introduction of hot showers and new toilets, in 1988 was a major improvement.

Towards the end of the eighties there was growing concern at Lee Abbey at the declining numbers of those coming to camp, and it was felt that major changes were needed. It was decided to split the camps with the first fortnight remaining as a two-week camp for sixteen- to twenty-five-year-olds, while the second fortnight was divided into two separate weeks with two dual-age group camps for thirteen- to fifteen-year-olds and sixteen- to nineteen-year-olds, with the two groups sharing together for meals, worship and some activities, but sleeping and being taught separately. For the first time a disco was part of the programme. Some team members, with long associations with camp, found these changes hard to accept, especially those involving the younger age group. Yet in 'Rapport', the Lee Abbey Newsletter, Fergus Macartney the lay chaplain responsible for the changes could report

> Scores of young people came out of darkness to make commitments to Jesus Christ, and just as many were filled with the Holy Spirit for the first time. The final communion services were stupendous celebrations of the love and faithfulness of God. How can I forget the sight of more than one row of around six young men quite unable to control the tears of joy pouring from their eyes! When strong lads like these abandon the need to be cool, then the Kingdom of God really is drawing near.

This continues to be the pattern for camp with Phil and Di Stone now leading the first camp following the retirement of Chris and Pat Rogers in 1992.

Whatever the elements that account for the profound impact of this camp, in the end the decisive factor is that it is founded on the work of God rather than the techniques of man. This has been demonstrated many times. On several occasions campers have come up to a member of the team after the Communion service on the first Sunday morning full of joy with the news that they have just surrendered their lives to Christ. Here is God at work, for no challenge has been put to them other than the words and experience of the Communion service itself! The atmosphere of the camp has a profound effect. One boy from a very unhappy home reflected, 'What means so much to me about this camp is the peace in this place.'

God's control of all that happens at camp has never been more dramatically demonstrated than in 1971. Early on in the first camp Ray had invited a new team member, Dave Gait, later to become leader of the second camp, to give the epilogue on the Holy Spirit. It was the first time that Dave had ever spoken in public and he was extremely nervous. This, combined with the fact that he was naturally softly spoken and had a strong Liverpudlian accent, meant that he was going to find it difficult to make himself understood! As soon as he began to speak, disaster struck, for it started to pour with rain, which thundered on the canvas of the marquee. Frantic signs from the back to speak up were of no avail; not even those sitting in the front row could hear a word of what he was saying!

As Dave finished speaking the rain stopped. His final sentence was the only one to be heard, 'If you feel that your Christian life is inadequate then come over to the chapel tent and we will pray about it.'

It appeared that the evening had been a fiasco. Why did God allow it to rain throughout the epilogue? Ray felt particularly despondent. Yet only a few minutes after the epilogue he heard some beautiful singing coming from the chapel tent. Picking his way across the field where the atmosphere was still heavy after the storm he came across a small circle of campers praying together and jumping up and down with joy. A little further on was another group, and in the chapel tent itself he found a large crowd singing together in tongues, praising God in the most glorious harmony. That evening can only be described as another Pentecost. In His sovereign power the Holy Spirit had descended upon the camp and touched many lives. The next day at the team meeting the camp's programme had to be hastily reorganised to provide suitable teaching for the large number of new Christians. Dave was asked to give the same epilogue during the second camp. He did, though it did not rain and the response was not repeated.

Only at the end of August did it become clear that the mighty blessing granted by God at that first camp was His preparation for a very difficult second camp. Before the camps began Ray received a word from God: 'You are to stand back and let the young ones do the witnessing.' He assumed this referred to him as leader and that God wanted the younger team members to play a larger part in the ministry. Dave's epilogue seemed to confirm this. However, it was a prophecy for the whole team.

The camp was proving difficult because of a number of campers with complex spiritual problems. About halfway through, Simon, one of the campers, went missing. Normally the police would not be over-concerned at news of a missing teenager, but this was different: Simon was epileptic. The field was filled with police, coastguards, a TV crew and even the Army. The routine of camp was abandoned as most of the team, together with older campers, became fully involved in the massive search operation. No sign was found until Thursday, when a track was discovered on the cliff edge near Hunters Inn, which indicated where he must have gone over the cliff. His body was never recovered.

Even in this tragedy, the hand of God was evident. Before he went missing Simon had acknowledged Jesus as Lord of his life. In the camp, with all the team out searching, the ministry was not allowed to suffer: with camper ministering to camper, another mighty work of the Holy Spirit took place. It was deeply humbling to the team to see the fulfilment of the earlier word to let 'the young ones do the witnessing'.

In the late 1950s a survey was conducted revealing that there were well over 200 people in full-time

Christian ministry who claimed that the Lee Abbey
Youth Camp had played a major part in their spiritual growth. There is no doubt that this number has
continued to increase with every camp.

Typical of many young people whose lives have been
transformed by God at camp was Chris, an apprentice
bricklayer from the West Country. It was at the suggestion of the curate of his local church, where he attended
the youth group, that Chris first went to camp in 1988.
He went alone and first impressions were not good.
His fellow campers seemed very different from his
colleagues on the building site. However, he quickly
made friends and had a good time, fully entering
into the life of the camp, except for the epilogues,
from which he kept a safe distance. One night he
had skipped the epilogue to go to the pub and on
returning found people being prayed for. He felt very
left out and frightened. However, he sensed that the
team members cared for him, and that they were not
pressurising him to conform. So, the next year he
returned to camp, though it was to be a very different
time. Work was becoming increasingly difficult and he
was very unhappy. Once again, he enjoyed the camp
activities to the full, but this time took the epilogues
more seriously. One night, Ray Fardon was visiting the
camp and spoke on the Holy Spirit. Chris responded
to the challenge and went to the chapel tent seeking
prayer. As he describes it, he 'stopped fighting and
gave in to God. I felt a great sense of peace and that
the building site didn't matter any more'.

When Chris returned to camp the next year it was
to be as a team member. He soon found that it was
altogether different from being a camper for he was
head 'lat man' responsible for emptying the latrines
at 5.30 a.m. each morning! For a young Christian the
experience of sharing in the team meeting was a great
encouragement deepening both his sense of expectation
of God and his personal prayer. Chris left the building

site and applied to join the Lee Abbey Community in London, where as a member of the maintenance team his practical skills were put to good use. He served on the camp team for a further two years until his marriage and now plays a full part in the life of his local church and is training for social work.

For some time now the culmination of every camp has been a Communion service on the final evening. After supper the marquee which has been dining room, meeting room and, as often as not, a shelter from the rain, is transformed. The sides of the tent and the central poles are swathed in leaves and ferns. Three chandeliers of candles provide light and at one end all the paraffin lamps are lit and assembled on a table. An atmosphere of great beauty is created with the scent of the greenery, the flickering candle-light and the glow of the pressure lamps. When everything is ready the campers are invited in. It is a breathtaking sight, a symbol for many of what the camp has come to mean to them – a green temple, a place for meeting with the living Christ.

During the service, there is an opportunity for any-body to come forward to receive a simple cardboard cross as a token of any step of faith taken during camp. This is an act of both will and emotion. Some do not wish to take a cross and are respected for that. However, there are many who do – a testimony to young lives touched by God.

As people greet one another and say farewell during the Peace, they acknowledge that during their time together God has made them into the Body of Christ. They go out to share in the wider body of the Church and of the world, which for many of them is going to be far from easy. For Lee Abbey there is deep thanksgiving that Christ has once again met with all those he has brought on to the field.

Chapter 10
More than a Happy Hotel?

'Does the Gospel people hear at Lee Abbey make heavy enough demands on them? . . .

'Does it invite people to go on in prayer, not to struggle to recapture their first experience but to let God take them on to the further reaches of fellowship with Him? . . .

'Does the Gospel proclaimed here at Lee Abbey invite people not to be content with easy answers to hard problems, but to love God with their minds? . . .

'Does the Gospel proclaimed here really invite people to take the world seriously as loved and redeemed by God, and as the only material for the making of His kingdom? . . .

'Does the Gospel proclaimed here send people away basically fearful and defensive or does it send them away hopeful, liberated, ready to take initiative?'

Geoffrey Paul was giving his last Warden's charge to the Community. This is an annual occasion on the Tuesday in Holy Week, when at the corporate Communion the red-label Community members renew their promises and the Warden shares with the Community something of what he senses God is saying. Geoffrey returned to a theme that had been one of his constant concerns during his five years as Warden. It remained an underlying question for the Community throughout the seventies.

More than a Happy Hotel?

For a regular visitor to Lee Abbey this was a time when there was little outward change. Letters continued to indicate the varied ways in which God was using Lee Abbey and blessing the ministry, yet there was an underlying sense of uncertainty within the Council and the Community. It was wrong to assume that just because the house was full with guests and they were being blessed, that therefore Lee Abbey was fulfilling its task.

Plenty of new people were coming, almost fifty per cent of the guests each year – but the majority were either committed Christians or those from a church background. Lee Abbey was no longer attracting people from outside church circles and although there were still many guests for whom the Gospel message was completely new, it was clear that the Community was not touching the unchurched masses. Some feared that the place was becoming just a very happy hotel providing spiritual refreshment for Christians, rather than an evangelistic centre.

This concern for the role of Lee Abbey influenced many of the major decisions that had to be made during this period; for example, the way that Lee Abbey reacted to the problem of inflation. The policy had always been to keep fees as low as possible, so the maximum number of people would be able to afford to come. Suddenly massive increases were required. For a few years the fees were kept down, but as it was realised that inflation was not going to stop, an increase of forty-two per cent was needed to account for VAT and to place the work once more on a sound financial footing. Keeping pace with inflation meant that fees rose from £10.10s. per week in 1970 to £64.00 per week by 1980. Inevitably there were people who could no longer afford to come, but the predicted drop in guest numbers did not take place. At the same time it became firm policy to increase bursaries so that financial aid was more freely available to help those often most in need of a break at Lee Abbey, who would otherwise be unable to afford the fees.

Money, however, was only one of the factors which determined who should come to stay. Even if the fees could be kept very low, many of those people whom the Community wished to reach would have found the whole environment of Lee Abbey totally alien to their way of life. There was no bar, grace was said before meals, the whole concept of a holiday houseparty was off-putting to many people. The question that faced the Community and the Council was whether Lee Abbey should accept that its ministry was limited, or should actively seek ways of reaching a wider group of people.

In the Lee Abbey structure the Warden is the key man in determining the nature of the Community's work. Two men, Geoffrey Paul and John Perry, held the post during the seventies and in making each appointment the Council were clearly seeking a man who would bring a fresh direction to the work.

Geoffrey Paul, Canon of Bristol Cathedral, replaced Ken Pillar, who moved in 1970 to become vicar of Waltham Abbey. Unlike Ken's appointment, six years before, which had been a closely guarded secret, this was far more open – even Friends were asked to send in names of people whom the Council might consider for the post. Geoffrey had made a great impression on the Chapter in Devon when he had come as guest speaker for the International Houseparty in 1969. Before moving to Bristol, where he was responsible for ordinands and post-ordination training, he had served for fifteen years in South India, spending much of that time teaching in a theological college. With his wife, Pam, and their five daughters, Geoffrey moved to Devon in July 1971. As at Ken's arrival, the Community found that they had to adjust to a very different style of leadership. After a period during which decision-making had become increasingly a corporate responsibility,

More than a Happy Hotel?

Geoffrey was very much a father figure both in leadership and as pastor and counsellor. To have as Warden a man who was at heart a theologian with a deep love of the Bible was a new and challenging experience. Ken had been anxious that guests should be encouraged to look outwards, away from a self-conscious personal religion to embrace the wider problems of society. Geoffrey, too, was concerned that Lee Abbey should be a place where people were challenged to consider their faith, and to return home to relate it both to their local church and to the world. Although healing and renewal continued to be a central part of Lee Abbey's ministry he stressed that, as in the ministry of Jesus, there must be a balance between meeting people's needs with God's revealing power, and challenging people in His strength to go and change the world. He was also concerned about the attitude of the Community to those who came to stay. There was a danger of seeing every guest in terms of a problem needing healing, counselling and propping up, rather than as a potential warrior for Christ, to be charged for a personal mission.

Geoffrey taught that the world should be taken seriously. As he wrote to the Friends,

> I suspect we too easily give encouragement to those who are afraid of, or a bit shocked by today's world, and do not do enough to encourage those who are fascinated by all the dangerous and wonderful power, ingenuity, imagination and inventiveness in every sphere of life that God has given to men, and who want to get in amongst it all to claim it as His and for Him. Are the Christians who go out from here sufficiently up at the front of change, reform and development, social economic and international?

To provide stimulation, alongside the Community pastoral team Geoffrey invited a much greater diversity of guest speakers than had come to Lee Abbey in the past. It was a deliberate attempt to bring a wider intellectual content and challenge to the teaching. It was a controversial policy provoking strong reaction from a number of guests and Community members, especially from those who were disturbed whenever the Gospel was not presented in traditional evangelical terms.

Geoffrey was anxious that the Community should attract people from outside the usual church-going belt to consider the claims of Christ, but it was not easy. In 1972 three houseparties were set aside, nicknamed 'Wild Weeks', with the aim of breaking away from the traditional programme structure and presenting the Gospel in more contemporary language. In the newsletter Friends were encouraged to bring along people who they knew would normally regard the idea of 'a religious holiday at a place like Lee Abbey' with horror. It was a bold idea but the response was very disappointing, for when the guests arrived it was clear that the majority were from Christian backgrounds and that links with the unchurched masses had not been made.

During this time Lee Abbey was breaking new ground in its ministry to guests through the use of the creative arts. Spearheaded by the Renewal Movement throughout the Church, there was a re-emergence of the arts – music, drama, art and poetry – both as a means of communication and as an expression of worship.

At Lee Abbey this was experienced in a highly original and at times unconventional way through two chaplains, Philip Humphreys and Doug Constable. Both were very gifted musicians and their approach sought to embrace a full range of musical traditions. Presentations became a regular feature of many houseparties, involving a large part of the Community; at times they were based on dramatic and musical material specially composed for the occasion. Themes as diverse as the plagues in Egypt, Job, and the history of the Lynton–Barnstaple railway were tackled. At Christmas the traditional Nativity tableau was replaced by a highly imaginative production. Guests, too, often found themselves caught up in a virtually spontaneous production which would be rehearsed and performed in the course of one evening. A 'Gospel and Arts' week became a regular addition to the houseparty programme. A whole new area of Christian expression was being opened up which challenged Community and guests to discover and use the full range of the arts in worship and evangelism – something that was happening throughout the Church – and also to be actively creative in composing, writing and painting.

These positive attempts to bring in new guests and explore different methods of communication re-established Lee Abbey as a centre for evangelism. Yet it was an approach to evangelism that was very different from that of the founders'. As the seventies progressed there were fewer and fewer links with the early days to remind the Community of the daring faith and vision which had been at its foundation.

Several events underlined this growing separation from the past. In 1974 Jack Winslow died. It was twelve years since he had retired from Community life to live in Godalming, but he had retained his passionate interest in Lee Abbey. His death was absolutely in keeping with his life.

In March 1974 at the age of 92, he decided to revisit India, the scene of his early ministry. Within forty hours of his arrival he found himself again preaching in Marathi, with the old fluency returning even after so many years. He revisited the ashram at Poona which he had founded in 1921 and discovered that after some years of decline it was developing strongly again in an ecumenical fellowship of the Spirit. The whole tour was one of great joy, as he had reunions with old friends, their sons and grandsons! A few days after his return to England, Jack went into hospital with symptoms of heart trouble; after receiving Holy Communion with the local vicar he died peacefully, at the completion of a long and very fruitful life.

The next year was the thirtieth anniversary of the purchase of Lee Abbey, with celebrations to give thanks to God for all that He had accomplished in Devon and London. They underlined both how much the work had developed, and also that it was now a different era for Lee Abbey. As for previous reunions, a large gathering was arranged in London with a Communion service at St Paul's Cathedral and a rally at the Royal Festival Hall. Over 1,400 people were present, but this was a mere shadow compared with the days when St Paul's had been packed to the doors, and the Festival Hall appeared to be less than half full. People no longer flocked to mass gatherings in the way that they had in the fifties. For the first time the seven men who had led the Community as Wardens, four in Devon and three in London, were brought together. Beginning with Roger de Pemberton, they traced the development of the work. Sitting alongside the seven clergymen on the platform was one woman, Madeleine Wheen, who as Lady Warden in Devon for twenty-eight years had served under each Warden in turn. By the time of the reunion she had already decided that she should retire. Without her presence some further change of direction was inevitable.

It seemed that the Community was only beginning to adjust to the changes resulting from Madeleine's departure when once again there was to be a new man as Warden. Geoffrey Paul had completed nearly six years at Lee Abbey when he was appointed to be Bishop of Hull. As his successor the Council chose John Perry with his wife Gay, a man who knew Lee Abbey well. He and his family had been coming as guests for over twenty years and on a number of occasions he had been a guest speaker. John and Gay had become

engaged there and together they had received a rich
blessing from the Holy Spirit while staying at Lee
Abbey in 1963.

On July 20th, 1977 Geoffrey Rogers spoke of the
enormous sense of expectancy in the air as Denis
Wakeling, now Bishop of Southwell and Chairman of
the Council, installed John as the fifth Warden and
welcomed John and Gay with their five children to
the Community. For the next twelve years they were
to shape the ministry of Lee Abbey. It was a strong
partnership, with John's authoritative and sensitive
leadership and Gay's particular gifts of welcoming
hospitality and friendship offered freely to guests and
Community members.

There seemed to be little doubt in anybody's mind
that the new Warden would bring big changes. As
Geoffrey had been appointed to bring theological weight
to the Community's ministry, John came from a parochial background. For the previous fifteen years he had
been vicar of St Andrew's, Chorleywood which under
his leadership had become well-known as a parish
greatly blessed through the Renewal Movement and
which had developed an effective evangelistic strategy
in its ministry.

A few years earlier it would have been unthinkable
for anybody with known charismatic connections to be
even considered for the post of Warden. The intention
had always been that Lee Abbey should be seen as
serving the whole Church, though in practice it was
very doubtful if that had been achieved for a long time;
a Warden identified with one particular party was not
thought to be a good idea. John's appointment reflected
not so much a major change of policy by the Council,
but an indication of the way that the new work of
the Holy Spirit was becoming recognised: not in the
creation of a new 'charismatic sect' but in bringing
renewed life to the mainstream churches. Those who
assumed that under John's leadership, Lee Abbey

would become an exclusively 'charismatic community' were to be wrong. John's vision was that Lee Abbey should continue to serve the whole Church. The basic concern remained the same – the continuing search to discover the real role that God wanted Lee Abbey to play as a centre for renewal and evangelism. Having valued Lee Abbey's ministry as a guest, and from his experience in Chorleywood, John had shared with the Council, before his appointment, two specific areas that he believed needed to be developed.

The first concern was the ministry to the guests who came to stay – the problem raised by the image of the happy hotel. In Geoffrey's time the keyword had been 'challenge', now it became 'encouragement'. In addition to the holiday houseparties where people could come away to relax and find renewal in body, mind and spirit, John believed that Lee Abbey had an enormous potential for training both clergy and lay people. It had always been part of Lee Abbey's agenda, but had never really been properly realised. While part of the attraction of Lee Abbey in the summer was its remoteness, the building of the motorways meant that it was now readily accessible in winter. John was concerned to maximise the winter months when, apart from weekends, and the period over Christmas, the house was little used.

For the first time in the winter of 1978/9 a conference programme was arranged, covering a wide variety of topics using both Community and guest speakers. It was to bring a whole new range of people to stay at Lee Abbey. As was expected, certain themes immediately proved popular. It could be guaranteed that a conference on healing, prayer or spirituality would always be well-supported. Given Lee Abbey's setting, rural ministry was an obvious theme. Links were developed with the caring professions, as conferences were mounted jointly with the Pain Society and the Hospice movement – the latter becoming a bi-annual event. There were however, some conferences that had to be cancelled for lack of support. These tended to be those concerned with social issues. It was a sharp indication to the Community that people did not see Lee Abbey as having a social agenda, or having much to say on these matters. While this criticism was probably unjustified, during the coming years, Lee Abbey also began to address them, reflecting the wider concern within the Renewal Movement to take these issues more seriously.

John Perry's other priority on becoming Warden, was the expansion of the Community's outreach work. At Chorleywood he had experienced the evangelistic effectiveness of faith-sharing teams, small teams of Christians going out from the church to share their faith and learn from other congregations. John believed that the Community was a rich resource for such evangelism. The Community already undertook two major ten-day missions each year; this mission programme was to be greatly expanded.

Since then there has not only been a steady increase in the number of missions undertaken each year by the Community, but there has been a defining and refining of outreach strategy. It has become increasingly clear that Lee Abbey's calling is not so much to lead missions, but to help create missionary churches; not to go into a parish to do their evangelism for them, but to provide the training and the encouragement that enables congregations to reach out with the Good News of Christ. The new emphasis on outreach from Lee Abbey meant that instead of having one chaplain with particular responsibility for overseeing the outreach programme, there is now a chaplain evangelist for whom this is their sole responsibility.

As a predominantly lay community of mixed Christian traditions and ages, Lee Abbey offered a broad-based mission team that was welcomed by groups of churches, such as deaneries, or councils of churches for whom the traditional theological college or religious community team would have seemed too narrow. Some missions were to cover quite large areas; one involved the whole island of Jersey. Large areas needed large teams, and while the creativity and youthful vitality of the team often inspired churches, it was also recognised that there was a need for older people to provide a balance. The answer was to draw on Friends – regarded by John as another under-used Lee Abbey resource. Involving Friends had a number of advantages; the breadth of experience could be strengthened, the pressure on the Community in Devon with people away was relieved; and more mission invitations could be accepted. Most Lee Abbey teams would now be made up of a core of members drawn from Lee Abbey in Devon and sometimes London, and a group of Friends, a number of whom might be former members of Community. According to their abilities the core team would seek to make full use of the gifts of drama, dance and music which were used in holiday houseparties in Devon. However, equally important was the use of personal testimony, for it is somebody telling their story of faith, not often dramatic or spectacular, that can convey the reality of Christ.

One Friend, who has been greatly used by God in this way is Frank who has been on a number of mission teams and has assisted at holiday houseparties. Frank was part of the team at a Follow-up Weekend in Coventry. During the Family Service at a local school he was interviewed about his life and faith. He described how he came from a broken home and had been taken into care when his mother could not cope. At the age of thirteen he went to a boys' camp where he gave his heart to Jesus. After the service a thirteen-year-old lad, Peter, came up to him and said that he also lived in a foster home and he would like to give his heart to Jesus. Promptly, a fourteen-year-old girl, Donna, from the same home said she wanted to do the same. Peter said he did not have a Bible so, after writing in it, Frank gave him his New Testament.

A mission to the Cotswolds in 1983 was to prove particularly effective. Canon Arthur Dodds had had links with Lee Abbey for many years. In his role as Rural Dean of North Leach he organised a mid-week Deanery Conference at Lee Abbey in November 1980. About eighty guests enjoyed the normal combination of Lee Abbey activities. During the week a number of people came to faith in Christ and there were those for whom their faith was renewed. The conference was repeated in several more years, with the result that relationships were being strengthened (across the Deanery). A letter from Arthur Dodds to John Perry asking about the possibility of a Lee Abbey mission to the Cotswolds literally crossed in the post with a letter from John suggesting the same idea to Arthur. A large team of Lee Abbey Community and Friends led a 'Celebration of Faith' in March in 1983. Three deaneries were involved and while there were to be few first-time commitments to Christ, the impact on the churches was to be profound, and the effect seen for many years. As a direct result of this contact with Lee Abbey, a group was to form Harnhill Manor in 1986 as a centre of Christian healing in the Cotswolds.

Yet experience showed that some missions could be too large. When a mission was initiated by a council of churches, it was easy for a number of churches to be identified with the mission, but not really committed to it. The result would be that the team's resources would be too thinly spread. It was congregations that were themselves committed to mission, who had prayed and looked for God to act, that were to know His blessing, while others felt disappointed that Lee Abbey had not brought them new church members.

It became clear that, if the Community was going to be effective, it needed to spend more time with churches preparing for missions. As a result, in addition to preparation meetings in the parish, a church requesting a mission team would be asked to bring a core group to share in a Lee Abbey groups' weekend, designed particularly for churches planning outreach. Here the opportunity would be taken to help churches develop their own mission strategy – in particular in developing long-term friendships and in challenging people to relate culturally to their local community.

This strategy has been further refined with a move away from the traditional ten-day mission period to a much longer period of involvement with a parish. Now a mission may involve a preparation weekend, followed by a five-day team visit from Wednesday to a Sunday, another weekend six months later, followed by a consultation meeting a year later. The Lee Abbey involvement with the church being over an eighteen-month to two-year period.

God's use of Lee Abbey teams was illustrated when an invitation for a visit from a mission team was received from a parish in South Devon. The invitation was received with little enthusiasm as a team had visited the parish six years before and had achieved little. They had returned despondent at the lack of response, having sensed spiritual darkness and apathy in the place. However, an initial visit was made. It was soon after Mike Edson had arrived as Warden and he was surprised to find the vicarage sitting-room packed with people for the special PCC meeting with a sense of eagerness and expectation of what God was going to do. He expressed his surprise and explained the reaction there had been in the Community. A church-warden explained that far from being a failure, it was the previous mission that had made him, and many others, start thinking seriously about the challenge to the Christian life for the first time. There had not been conversions, but the Lee Abbey team had been a catalyst to the beginning of a whole new work of God.

* * *

The development of the conference programme and the expansion of outreach was not to be at the expense of the holiday houseparty ministry, which continued to be the backbone of the work of Lee Abbey. For guests Lee Abbey continued to have the same attraction. Here was a Christian place where you could be free to do what you wished without the pressure to attend the whole programme. A couple could come together on holiday even when one was not a Christian, and yet each partner enjoy the place in their own way. It was this freedom, which is often claimed but rarely experienced, that time and time again was to be pinpointed as such a blessing. Lee Abbey was also a good place for a family holiday. By appointing full-time children and youth workers during the summer months there was a wide range of activities for both children and young people.

A full programme of houseparties, a new winter conference programme and more outreach teams could not be sustained by the Community as it was. John realised that it would be necessary to keep the Community at full strength throughout the year, rather than, as before, to reduce numbers in the winter months during which there had been a long period closed to guests. There was also the much more sensitive issue of selection of Community members and here there was to be a significant change.

Countless men and women since 1945 can testify to a year or two on the Lee Abbey Community as being a time of great spiritual growth and healing. People with experience of Lee Abbey have often suggested to young people, perhaps going through a difficult period, that they might spend time at Lee Abbey. John believed that God's calling to Lee Abbey was to serve the Church and the guests who came, and not to serve itself. When the Community became inward looking, pre-occupied with its own problems, it would be losing its vision. The call to Lee Abbey was to serve. That was not to say that the search was on for perfect Community members. It will continue to be only those who know for themselves the forgiving, healing power of God in their lives and their continuing need of that, who will be able to minister to others, but those same people have to be those who are willing to serve others and not just themselves.

Community life was demanding in both time and energy, yet it was also rewarding. For many it was a time of growing in faith and, often much to their surprise, discovering new abilities and talents. It also involved much fun and laughter. The Lee Abbey Community continues to be a place where deep friendships are formed, many lasting long after people have moved on. It has also been a place where romance has blossomed, though here great care has always been needed and there has been an important rule that if a couple wish to become engaged to be married then one of them must leave the Community in order to test the relationship.

Today the Lee Abbey Community continues to be made up of a mixture of families and young people. In 1995 there are seven families on the Community including eight children and forty-three single Community members. In addition to those from Britain, there are members from Germany, Holland, Sweden, Poland, the USA, Canada, South Africa, Japan, and with the opening up of the Eastern Bloc, Albania, Hungary and the Ukraine.

While there was no shortage of applications for Community membership, a real problem arose in finding relevantly skilled people. Sophisticated equipment and ever more stringent Health and Safety Regulations increasingly required qualified people to work in the kitchen, and computerisation necessitated skilled people to work in the offices to a degree that had not been needed in the past. For effective witness the Community needed members who were eager to grow in faith in Christ, but this witness also had to involve the efficiency of the booking office, the quality of meals

and the care of the house and grounds. God continued
to bring the right people to the Community, often as
a result of concerted prayer for a caterer, a chef, a
computer programmer, or somebody skilled in milking
cows, and Lee Abbey continued to be a place where
people learnt new skills and flexibility in working;
yet it was a strained and sometimes inefficient way
to work.

There was also a growing problem of continuity. On
average a younger Community member stays for one to
two years, with thirty-five per cent of the Community
changing each year. This is the nature of Lee Abbey,
but it means that the departmental work teams, and
even their leaders, are frequently changing. The situation was not helped by a time of growing national
unemployment. Experience has shown that in times of
high unemployment Community members will be more
reluctant to extend their time, because of their concern
to enter into a long-term career. Sadly, membership of
a Christian community is regarded with considerable
suspicion by potential employers.

These problems were focused in the kitchen. When
the house was full, which it was for much of the year,
the kitchen team would be catering for almost 200
people, for three meals a day, seven days a week. There
seemed to be an almost continual staffing crisis, for all
this work could not be sustained by amateurs, however
willing and enthusiastic.

Increasingly the question was being raised whether
all the work necessary for the efficient running of the
house could or should be undertaken by the Community members alone.

The solution was to bring in more outside workers to
fill the key posts: local people, who would be employed
to do a normal week's work. They would not be Community members, though it was essential that they were
in sympathy with the work of Lee Abbey.

This was not a totally new idea. Many years before

it had been decided that outside workers needed to be employed to do the ongoing maintenance work which the large building required. With their blue labels, the outside workers were an important part of Lee Abbey, and both Harold Fradgley and Johnny Stiling have now been working at Lee Abbey for almost twenty-five years. This policy of employing outside people was now extended, with people brought in to undertake key roles in both the kitchen and the office. The decision removed a major pressure point on the Community and the 'pink labels', as they were identified, provided the much-needed continuity and skill to enable the Community members to do their work well.

This decision raised new issues about the nature of community. Is it a sign of weakness and failure when Christians have to accept and draw on the skills of others? Does God call His people, whether in a church or a community to be self-sufficient? At Lee Abbey it is a further challenge to the Community's witness in relationships. Now as well as relationships with each other and with guests there is the working out of relationships between pink labels and Community members: a particular challenge when a Community member is new to Lee Abbey and the pink label has been working at Lee Abbey for many years.

However, this is the very challenge that many Christians are needing to face in their workplace, and where so often Christian witness is severely compromised.

Chapter 11
Under One Roof

C hristian people are called to be a pilgrim people.
The New Testament presents Abraham as the
example of the man of faith, for whom obedience to
God meant always being on the move – pitching his
tents, and then moving on. Few find such obedience
easy; it is even harder for Christian congregations and
organisations. As the seventies drew to a close, there
was little doubt in most people's minds as to where God
was leading Lee Abbey in Devon, but in London it was
very different. In the next few years it was the future
direction of the work of the Lee Abbey International
Students' Club that was to preoccupy the Lee Abbey
Council.

It was a time of rapid change in the student situation
in London. Government cutbacks in grants meant that
the boom of overseas students in the sixties was truly
over. Increasingly it was only students from wealthy
countries who could afford the fees and were able
to come and study in England. So the majority of
students seeking accommodation were now from the
Middle East, Malaysia and Singapore rather than the
poorer African countries and the West Indies. Such
students came with very different needs. They expected
high standards of accommodation. They brought the
problems of wealth, not of poverty.

At the same time the four hotels that made up
Lee Abbey in London were becoming increasingly
dilapidated. Since the opening of the Club only crisis

maintenance had been carried out on the Victorian buildings and they were now showing their age, with antiquated heating and plumbing, and drab decoration. It was not a welcome place either to live or to work, and it was not cheap.

This changing situation produced a crisis in the Community. The job was very different from the initial vision. Was God really calling Lee Abbey to offer sub-standard accommodation to wealthy students? Soon after the Club was established it was realised that the task of the Community in London was altogether different from that of Devon. Successive Wardens had stressed the need for mature committed Community members who would stay for several years. While the Club was well served by a number of just such people throughout the seventies yet in reality the majority of the Community were comparatively young in faith and age and did not find it easy to relate to students.

In 1977 there was a clear deterioration in resident Community relations; with a succession of complaints often focused on food and standards of accommodation. At the Council weekend, with morale low in the Club, David Johnson, who had succeeded Chris Hayward as Warden in 1974, presented a frank paper analysing the situation as he perceived it. In essence he recommended that the Club had fulfilled its purpose from God and that it was time to close down. The Council however could not accept this recommendation – it was too committed to the work in London and did not believe that God was calling them to abandon the vision of ministry to overseas students. The decision was made that the Club's mission should continue.

When David Johnson moved to a new post later that year, the Council's response to his paper was to appoint Derek Barnes, a member of the West London Chaplaincy, a man with plenty of experience of ministry amongst students, as the new Warden. At the same time it was decided to strengthen the pastoral

work of the Club by appointing a lay chaplain, Lionel
Fernando, a Methodist Christian from Sri Lanka. He
would have particular responsibility for pastoring the
residents, freeing Derek to give more time to the Community. With enthusiasm Lionel and Derek initiated
a number of projects such as re-orientation courses to
help residents analyse their British experiences and be
able to use them when they got home. Despite these
initiatives the fundamental problems of the Club were
not stemmed. The buildings continued to decay and
student numbers continued to fall. By 1980/81 there
were 140 residents compared to 189 in 1974/5.

The crunch came in 1981 when, on his marriage,
Derek moved and John Watson was appointed as
Warden. John was altogether different from his predecessors – an Anglican priest, he was steeped in the
orthodox tradition of prayer and spirituality. Coptic
monks and Orthodox Bishops visiting the Club were
now pictured in *Rapport* – the Lee Abbey Newsletter.
John had a clear vision to deepen the spiritual life of
the Community, without which he believed the work
could not be sustained. After six months John voiced
what many had already concluded, that the basis
of David Johnson's paper was right, and that Lee
Abbey's mission in London with its present structures
and buildings could not continue. Two issues had to
be faced: the future of the present buildings, and the
structure of the Community, which John considered
was unable to undertake the task.

Management consultants were brought in to assess
the building and present the options. They reported
what everybody realised. Not merely were the buildings shabby and dilapidated in their decoration but
recent renovation work to the Compass Room had
revealed serious defects in the wiring system and there
were major structural problems with the kitchens. This
was in addition to the problem that had been there
from the outset, of having four separate buildings

which were necessarily inefficient and uneconomic. The management consultants produced a full range of options: one building could be sold and the money used to refurbish the others; all the buildings could be sold either to build a purpose-built hostel, or to purchase another hotel; the decision could be made to move out of London to meet student needs in the provinces; or they could sell up and the work be disbanded. John encouraged Council and management to look at all the options, but only after establishing the vision. They needed to find a building to fit the vision, not tailor the vision to the building. Careful research was done to establish the current needs of overseas students, but it was difficult to come by hard facts. There was clearly a surplus of hostel beds in Central London, but the suggestion that the demand was now for married self-catering accommodation was not proven. There was a strong conviction that Earls Court was the area in which God was calling Lee Abbey to serve students and there was a considerable reluctance to move too far away. The decision was taken to sell all the existing buildings and purchase another property. It was an immensely complex task. One of the most vital things was that all the Club's buildings should be sold to one person on the same day so that a direct move could be made to buy the new building, without having to close Lee Abbey, thus leaving all the residents homeless. An additional complication was that the Club in fact consisted of eight properties, not four, six of which were leasehold and only two freehold.

The search for a new property was not to be so difficult. With the closure of the West London Air Terminal there were many hotels in the area for sale. The Administrator, Steve Salisbury, was asked to visit a number of potential properties on behalf of the Management Committee. It was Steve who first visited the Suncourt Hotel in Lexham Gardens in April 1982. It was barely five minutes walk away from the present

Club buildings but was in a street that Steve had never visited before. On his first sight of the outside of the building Steve had the conviction that this was to be the new home for the Lee Abbey Club – a brief tour as a prospective guest confirmed this. It consisted of six Victorian houses. There were spacious public rooms. There were a number of single rooms for which there was a great demand among students. There was an updated heating system and a great bonus – a garden. There was no doubt that this was the property that Lee Abbey should seek to purchase.

The next months were to be taken up with fraught legal negotiations. The Housing Association that had initially agreed to purchase the present buildings withdrew their offer when their government grant was withdrawn. It was discovered that there was another party interested in the Suncourt Hotel, and Lee Abbey's bid had to be increased. Through the skill of Steve Salisbury, Anthony Harman, chairman of the Management Committee and Lee Abbey's solicitors, Paddy and Anne Marsh, all the necessary negotiations were successfully completed. All this had to be conducted with a considerable degree of secrecy. Consequently although the students and most Community members were told that the Club was to move they could not be told the new location. To put them in the picture Anthony Harman took all those who would still be members of the Community at the time of the move to stay in the Suncourt Hotel and so it was as hotel guests that most of the Community were first to see the premises.

Steve Salisbury co-ordinated the move. Ill health had forced John Watson to resign as Warden, and now Steve was acting-Warden. There were last-minute hitches. One student made trouble by refusing to move out and it was only a week before the sale that he was finally persuaded to leave. Some residents in Lexham Gardens formally objected to the replacement of the hotel by an overseas student hostel. September 6th had to have the planning of a military operation. Community prayers were at 6.00 a.m. Each Community member was responsible for seeing that eight residents got up early and had all their baggage packed. Only one overslept! If financial penalties were to be avoided, precisely at 9.00 a.m. every student had to have left the premises with all their luggage. Within three days everything else had to be moved to the new premises. Some residents helped with the move. Sheila Harman and Sheila Mayo took those with nothing better to do down to Brighton for the day. When the residents returned at 5.00 p.m. to the new Lee Abbey International Students' Club in Lexham Gardens the work was complete. That evening a Thanksgiving Service was held in the lounge led by the first Warden, Gordon Mayo. Everything had gone smoothly and everyone was very conscious that the hand of God had again guided Lee Abbey through some very turbulent and anxious months and days.

It was on April 9th 1983 that the new Club premises were officially opened by Lord Belstead, the Minister of State for Foreign and Commonwealth affairs, and dedicated by Denis Wakeling, chairman of the Lee Abbey Council. In his address Bishop Denis reminded those present, who represented the wide range of people involved in the work and ministry of Lee Abbey, of the initial purposes of the place.

From the first we have identified our primary task as providing residential accommodation for overseas students with the help of a Christian community. Both the provision of acceptable accommodation and the presence of a Christian community are essential to our task. If we don't provide acceptable accommodation no students will come and stay with us. And if this was just overseas student accommodation without any opportunity for Christian work no one would join the Community. The Christian Community here will seek to preach the Gospel by the sincerity of its life, the quality of its service and its readiness to answer for its faith when necessary.

It was not just the Club buildings that were dedicated that day, for the service included the installation of the new Warden. The Council had appointed Mike and Sue Battison to succeed John Watson. As God had provided a new building, so it was equally clear that He had provided the right person to take over leadership of the new Lee Abbey International Students' Club. Mike and Sue had plenty of experience of work with students. They had worked in Kenya, Uganda and Nigeria and had long links with the Lee Abbey movement, being involved with the leadership of the summer camps for many years, and for the past five years Mike being lay-chaplain in Devon and Sue the caterer. They were ideally suited for the task. It was with a realisation of God's faithfulness in difficult times and expectation of what was going to lie ahead that everybody sang 'All I have needed thy hand hath provided, Great is thy faithfulness, Lord unto me'. That faithfulness was going to be well tested during the coming years.

* * *

Despite the tremendous amount of sorting out that needed to be done, the move transformed the morale of the Community. Community and students alike enjoyed the vastly superior facilities, and there was a real sense that after so much uncertainty, secrecy and upheaval, God had reaffirmed the vision for Lee Abbey's work in London and the way ahead was clear. Activities to bring together Community and students such as Thursday Coffee Evenings and Bible studies were resumed almost immediately. While being under one roof had enormous practical advantages, there had been a fear that it would destroy the family spirit that the four houses of the old Club had created. The fear was to be unfounded.

Mike and Sue Battison were to bring a very different style of leadership. The relationship between Devon and London had become strained over the previous few years and though the Devon Community had sought to be supportive, there was an uneasy atmosphere between them. Coming from the Devon Community Mike could almost immediately transform this. They knew the people, and they also shared the same positive evangelistic vision.

However, John Watson's concern for Lee Abbey had not just been about the building. As he challenged the Management Committee on the state of the building, he had also presented far-reaching proposals about the nature of the Community. He believed that as presently conceived the Community was not able to do the task asked of them. He had proposed a radical reduction in Community numbers, seeking to establish an older, long-term core of Community members with much of the day-to-day practical work being done by outsiders. Mike did not wish to pursue these plans, but rather set about rebuilding the Community following the current pattern of working. Meanwhile God was bringing men and women to the Club who were to play a crucial part in its work. One such was Sonny, a Shi'ite Muslim from Iran. She had been a resident at the Club for several months where she witnessed the communal life of the Community. Despite great hostility from other Muslim residents she took the decision to become a Christian and was baptised by John Watson after joining the Community. At the end of 1994, after thirteen years of service at the club she joined the staff of the International Fellowship of Evangelical Students. Another person to come to faith was Simon Mason – a research student in naval history. It was the London University accommodation list that first put

Simon in touch with Lee Abbey. At the time he had no idea what Lee Abbey was about, but it was offering the sort of accommodation that he was seeking. Although Simon came from a church-going background, he had decided that the Christian faith was not for him. It was witnessing the life of the Community rather than any concerted evangelistic presentation that was to challenge Simon to Christian commitment. What was believed was being shown and declared in daily life. Christian faith was being demonstrated in the attitude of Community both to each other and to the residents. Three years later Simon was himself to join the Community and to play a major part in the ministry of Lee Abbey.

Mohammad came to stay at Lee Abbey in 1984, to continue his Business Studies course. He was born a Muslim in Iran but most of his education had been in England. When he arrived at the Club he was in difficulty with the Home Office over his immigration status. He was under considerable pressure and he found the Christian presence of the Club deeply disturbing. During the summer he visited the Summer Camp in Devon and was invited to an open meeting of a John Wimber Conference in October. The preaching was powerful and the effect on people's lives all over the hall was evident. As he was leaving he was asked, 'How do you react to what you have seen tonight?'. 'I need peace,' he replied. 'Would you like us to pray for the peace of Jesus to enter your life?'. 'Yes please.' His life began to become more peaceful, if more complex. His appeal to the Home Office was rejected; the pressure increased. Mohammad was asked to join a small study group interested in learning more about the basic beliefs of Christianity. Two Community members were running this and some half dozen or so met regularly in the early part of the year. On July 14th 1985 he was baptised in a local church and severed his links with the past, taking the name of John.

However, there are also examples of lives that were not to be changed. In *Rapport* of April 1985 Mike wrote about 'Jon'. Jon was not a student, but one of many young people drawn into the shadowy life of drugs, prostitution and theft in Earls Court. During the summer of 1984 Jon came face to face with Christ through a street ministry evangelistic effort. His body was healed and his desire for drugs disappeared without withdrawal.

> Now there was a battle joined: to follow the signs and rebuild life anew; or to use this power to alleviate unpleasant symptoms while retaining old lifestyle and standards. Jon stayed at Lee Abbey for Christmas, and in the few weeks that followed, many Community and residents alike ministered friendship and hope, and encouragement to seek God's will in the chaos of his life. When he was due to leave he was offered a clear choice between the security of a Christian family and the road from there to rehabilitation and new life, or a return to the streets. The care had been consistent; the prayer had been persistent, and the love had been real in its concern, and constructive in its direction; and yet Jon chose the streets.

While the new building made life so much easier for the Community and residents yet it was the rebuilding of the Community which was to be critical for the fulfilment of the Lee Abbey vision. This was the calling to lifestyle witness. Firstly the calling 'to be' – to be seen as Christians; people who got tired and irritable and got on each others' nerves just like anybody else but who were yet committed to each other in love. The calling 'to do' – the sheer hard work of cooking and cleaning, answering the phone, sorting out a blocked toilet or a temperamental lift – often monotonous and repetitive. And the calling 'to speak out' – not afraid

when asked to give an account of faith to say 'This is
what I believe'. In one sense this is the calling of every
Christian, but at Lee Abbey it is being lived out very
publicly – 365 days each year in full view of people,
most of whom are from non-Christian countries, and
who are being taught to be intellectually critical.

When a person joins the Community of Lee Abbey in
London, as in Devon, after three months they can take
their Community promises to become full members. At
that Service they pray a prayer of personal commitment.

> Lord God, I am not my own, but yours.
> Put me to any tasks you have for me.
> Rank me with whom you will.
> Let me be employed for you, or laid aside
>   for you.
> Give me great responsibility, or little.
> Let me have everything, or nothing, except the
>   love of Christ
> and the power of the Holy Spirit,
> for Jesus' sake. Amen.

Despite the relief of leaving the old Club premises, there
was no illusion that the move to Lexham Gardens would
mean the end of building and maintenance work for the
Community. Even before the move, it had been decided
that the first project would be to clear the accumulated
rubbish from the basement to create a TV room, a
sports room and additional bedrooms. It was also going
to be necessary to relocate and re-equip the kitchen and
servery to make it more practical for self-service meals.
With financial help from the Lee Abbey Friends, much
of this work was to be completed within the first year.

The next major project was the roof. The surveyor's
report before the purchase of the building had indicated
that work on the roof would be needed – a reminder
that this was another Victorian building. As attention
was turned to this work two options were presented

to the Management Committee: the roof could simply be replaced, or, for comparatively little additional cost, the opportunity could be taken to rebuild the fourth and fifth floors, providing additional rooms – and so income – and upgrading the present accommodation. The issues were discussed, and Mike and the Management Committee had little doubt that they should take the opportunity to extend the fourth and fifth floors. If they had known at the time what this project would entail, it would have been with much greater trepidation that the decision was made, but that of course is what is involved in living a life of faith.

In 1989 Mike and Sue Battison completed their time as Warden, and moved to continue in student ministry in South Africa. Residents and Community were well-settled in the new building; the Community was strong, relations with Devon were good, there was a sense that this was God's work, and He was blessing it. To succeed Mike and Sue, the Council appointed David Littlefair, a parish priest from Plymouth, and his wife Christine, who, like Mike and Sue, had strong links with Lee Abbey through the Summer Camps. They had both lived in East Africa, and had had experience of work with students. Before ordination, David had been an accountant and they were a couple of great faith in the goodness and provision of God. God was providing qualities of leadership that were going to be needed and fully tested in the coming years.

Autumn 1989 marked the 25th anniversary of the establishment of the Lee Abbey Club in London. It was decided to mark the occasion with a great gathering of all involved in the ministry of Lee Abbey, at the Central Hall, Westminster – the first such gathering since the 30th anniversary celebration in 1976. Twelve hundred people including many ex-Community guests and Friends came for a day of teaching and celebration. It was a good opportunity too for many people to meet the two new Wardens – Mike Edson in Devon and

David Littlefair in London, and during the course of the worship they, along with Audrey Martin-Doyle were commissioned for their work by the Bishop of Coventry, chairman of the Council. The night before, as preparations were being made in Central Hall for the celebration, a gale was blowing in Central London. Community members at the Club struggled to hold down the plastic sheeting that now shrouded the roof of the building in an attempt to prevent damage, as water cascaded down into the third-floor Community and student bedrooms. For a time it even seemed that the scaffolding itself was in danger of collapse. It was a picture of the struggle that Lee Abbey in London was about to encounter.

The impact of the roof project was to be far greater than anyone had ever imagined, and was even to threaten the viability of the Club to continue in its ministry. As in any major building project it had been assumed that there would be unforeseen hitches; a bowing in the back wall of the building was revealed and this had to be secured. The cost increased from the contract price of £840,000 to an eventual total of over £900,000. What had not been anticipated, was that the contractors and consultants would not perform according to expectation. As a result the job suffered severe delays, and six months work became thirteen. Out of the Club total of 180 beds, 56 were lost while the work was being carried out, but as the work was still not completed for the beginning of the next academic year their loss stretched to a second year. Together with the unattractive image of the scaffolding and sheeting and the general atmosphere of a building site, Lee Abbey did not look very attractive to potential students. It was to take quite some time, even once the work was completed, to fill the new bed spaces. On top of these problems it was a period when interest rates were rocketing. As a result, by the autumn of 1990 Lee Abbey faced a severe financial crisis. What was God saying to the Community in all this? The

173

decision to go ahead with the project had been made prayerfully and carefully. Nobody believed that after the clear hand of God in the move to Lexham Gardens He was going now to allow this work in London to cease. The whole situation sapped the morale of the Community but under David's leadership there was a tremendous sense of tenacity that this was a problem that would have to be faced and resolved.

It was decided that the situation should be presented to the Lee Abbey Friends, though with the vast sums of money involved it was not with great confidence. Friends had already contributed to the appeal for the basement project, and in reality most of the Lee Abbey Friends' experience was of the work in Devon, not London. Had the work involved the homeless or the mentally handicapped that might have been different, but was there really a passionate concern for the needs of overseas students? Bishop Simon, chairman of the Council, and Eddie Shirras, chairman of the Management Committee, spearheaded the appeal. The target was £500,000 – only that sum would reduce the bank loan sufficiently to make interest payments manageable. Everybody realised it was a very large sum, but the Lee Abbey Friends responded wonderfully. Within a year David was able to report that £500,000 had been contributed through many people's generosity. There was a strong sense that again God had been faithful in providing for His work.

David Littlefair's skill as an accountant was to be fully used during his time as Warden, yet the true work of the Club continued and God was continuing to bless the ministry among students. One person who was to demonstrate the grace of God to Community and residents alike was Rosalind Cheng. Ros came from Singapore to the Club as a Law student in 1988. As a deeply-committed Christian she was soon joining in the prayer life of the Community and working in the kitchen to supplement her income. She became a member of the Community in 1990 and threw herself completely into the life of the Club. She was a great encourager of both students and Community members. She was eager to know God, and encouraged the Community in prayer and reading the Bible. Soon, however, she was asking for prayer for herself, as a cancer, previously thought to be cleared, re-appeared and spread rapidly. The Community fasted and prayed for Ros's healing, and with her could not understand why the Lord was not making her better. Ros did not get better, and in her last weeks she was nursed by the Community to within thirty hours of her death. In spite of her terrible suffering during those last few months she testified to God's wonderful healing of emotions, past hurts and relationships as her illness was used by Him to bring reconciliation within her family and the Community. Her step-sister Eileen came to faith in Christ and after Ros's death was baptised by David in the chapel at Lee Abbey in Devon. The Community knew that they had witnessed a great work of God's healing grace, though as so often, not in the way that they had expected. Ros's life and death had a profound effect on the Community, and in her memory the maintenance team built a terrace in the garden.

This was also a time of great political turmoil in the wider world, and as an International Students' Club with residents from all over the world, political upheavals were not just of academic interest. It was no exaggeration when somebody said that there was not a thing that was reported in the newspapers that didn't relate to somebody in the Club. For example it was the Middle East students who were to be the most vulnerable as the ongoing tensions in their own countries were highlighted in the Club. During the Iran/Iraq war an Iraqi Community member, a former militia man, who had come to faith in a Lebanese jail was sharing a room with an Iranian. When the

Americans shot down an Iranian airliner in 1988 not only were there a number of Iranian residents but a member of the Community was actually an American sponsored by the United States Air Force, taking a break in England. The whole chapel was in tears as they prayed together in the Communion Service that week.

The Gulf War of 1991, with students in residence from many Arab nations could have been felt no more intensely anywhere in London than at the Lee Abbey Club. There was the anxiety of what was going to happen. There were students, most of whom had done their compulsory National Service, expecting to be recalled to serve on either side in the conflict. The issues were hotly debated. There was the pain of the Iraqis for whom the great reality was that it was their homeland, their country, their family that was being bombed. At this time the Club was to offer a secure environment in which all those involved could be loved and supported by people from a whole variety of nations. One Iraqi Muslim student threatened with deportation sought the Community's help. His case was successfully presented to the Home Secretary. He said that never before had he experienced such love and concern as the Community had given. Lee Abbey was a true International Students' Club. It was for just such times that God had called it into being.

After five years as Warden, in 1994 David and Christine Littlefair moved to Wiltshire on David's appointment as vicar of Malmesbury Abbey. To succeed them, the Council appointed David and Jean Weekes.

After a curacy in Cheshire, they had worked in Uganda, during the tense time of Idi Amin's seizure of power. They then returned to Scotland where David became Chaplain and Head of Religious Studies at Fettes College in Edinburgh, and in due course Jean Housemistress for girls. There was a strong international aspect to their work.

176

Today, in 1995, the Club is again well filled with students, though changing patterns means that many more students today come for short term courses. However, underlying problems remain; issues concerning the nature of the Community, relationships with students, the care of the building, now twelve years older than when it was purchased and the provision of adequate funding. There is the constant need to keep the vision in focus – that the Club exists to minister to international students of all faiths. David and Jean are seeking ways of bringing this clear vision and the reality of the situation closer together.

Lee Abbey in London has learnt many lessons from God in the last thirty years of which the greatest is His faithfulness and the confidence of His continuing calling to serve overseas students in His name.

Chapter 12
A Fragile Stronghold

It was the second Sunday in December 1981. This is about the quietest time of the year at Lee Abbey in Devon for, with the house closed to guests, many members of the Community are away visiting family and friends before Christmas. It had been very cold for several days. While the members of the Community were having lunch a blizzard was raging, and the noise of the wind was so great that nobody realised what was happening outside. Within a period of twenty minutes large areas of the estate were reduced to a picture of complete devastation by hurricane winds of 120–160 miles per hour. It seemed that everywhere there were trees that had been uprooted or literally broken in half; every road and path was blocked; 150-year-old mature oak trees had been almost lifted out of the ground. Twenty-four acres of Douglas firs were completely flattened. Much of Cuddycleeve Wood between the North Walk and the sea was flattened. The Lee Abbey Estate was no longer a place of beauty, but chaos.

Yet God had protected. Nobody was injured. No building other than some portable toilets by the beach had been damaged, yet everywhere were fallen trees. It was to take until Christmas Eve even to clear the path to Jenny's Leap, and it was to take years to clear the remainder. The Community reacted with shock. The view down to the Bay would never be the same again, for the top of Bonhill, the hill that arises above Lee Bay, was now bare of trees. Yet there were new

vistas to enjoy as much more of the beach could now
been seen from the house.

It was a living parable, and was to provide a rich
fund of illustrations of the work of God for several years
to come. It was another example of God's protection,
yet the reasons for the extent of the devastation were
significant: the extreme cold had meant that the trees
were frozen so that when the storm came they had
been unable to bend with the wind. Also the wind had
come from the opposite direction from the prevailing
wind against which the trees for many years had put
down strong roots. A major programme of clearing and
replanting had to be undertaken, but gradually new life
began to spring from the dead stumps, and a new view
was to emerge which again would catch the breath and
inspire the artist and the photographer.

During the 1980s Lee Abbey was very much a mirror of the country. It was the time of Thatcherism,
of prosperity for some, and Lee Abbey enjoyed that
prosperity. For holiday houseparties the house was
full and it was even necessary to limit the number of
times people were allowed to visit each year during the
most popular times, and there was a steady increase
in numbers of those coming in the winter months. The
prosperity was reflected in the buildings.

Much of the Community accommodation had been
very poor, and with the need to encourage more
longer-term Community members, John Perry saw the
improvement of this as a priority, making it possible
for all full Community members to have their own
room. At last the 'horse boxes' and 'rabbit hutches',
which had been built as temporary accommodation for
the hotel staff in the 1920s, were replaced. A sports
hall was built and dedicated to the memory of Jack
Winslow. The old games and table-tennis room in the
back yard was enlarged to become a meeting room, to
take pressure off the octagonal lounge for meetings.

In building work it was what was not done that

was probably most significant at this time. Since the earliest days of Lee Abbey there had been plans to build a chapel on the North Lawn – a room that would be large enough to hold all Community and guests together. This need remained, for there was still no one place that could comfortably hold everyone together for Sunday morning worship or a Community presentation. Several plans had been drawn up for this North Lawn project. Yet John had no vision for it. It was not that money would have been a problem – Lee Abbey was a venture of faith, and experience taught that if something was the call of God then the money would be provided. A purpose-built conference hall and chapel could have been a great asset, for the new Preston Room tended to be cramped. It would however, have changed the atmosphere of the building. John was concerned to develop what God had already given Lee Abbey by making full use of existing buildings, in much the same way as the chapel had been created in 1951 by amalgamating three bedrooms, rather than embarking on an ambitious building project. Lee Abbey was to remain in essence the home of a Christian community and not become a hi-tech conference centre.

There was little outward change in the programme of the holiday weeks which ran from May to October. A holiday at Lee Abbey continued to have the same basic ingredients. In the morning there would be an opportunity for worship, a teaching session, usually led by a guest speaker, and perhaps the opportunity to share in a workshop discussion group. In the afternoon there was the opportunity to share in familiar walks, to Dean Farm or Croscombe Barton, along the coastal path to Hunter's Inn, or to Watersmeet, and for the more energetic to go further afield on Exmoor. After dinner there would be a programme of relaxing activities with perhaps the chance to try out a new hobby in an interest group, concluding with the evening epilogue.

As Lee Abbey benefitted from the prosperity of the eighties, it also found itself increasingly ministering to the casualties of that prosperity, and the fragmented society that was emerging. Lee Abbey was an ideal environment for one-parent families and there was a noticeable increase of these in many holiday weeks, often with financial assistance from the Bursary Fund. Such was the need, that a special one-parent-family week became a regular feature of the summer with a full programme of activities for children. It was an ideal place for people to unwind and find God's healing strength.

One of the great benefits of the programme for this particular week was not only that it gave the opportunity for the parents to have space from their children, and allow themselves to concentrate on their own needs, but it also gave the children and young people a unique opportunity to be themselves in a safe and secure environment. Many tears were shed, as deep healing took place, and very different children and parents left Lee Abbey to those who had arrived.

Anne Townsend, a guest speaker at a one-parent-family week spoke of her experience when she wrote:

Last year when we ran a week like this, one of the guests knelt at my feet at the closing Communion service. Her arms circled me, and her hair covered her face. I could feel as well as hear the pain in her choked whisper: 'Please pray for me ... I can't go on bringing up two babies on my own any longer ...' My heart wasn't the only one in the chapel that nearly broke in empathy with her pain. She was back again this year. She almost ran to greet me. 'Anne, it's true what I learned last year. God does love. God has seen me through. I am special to Him.'

There was the impact on children as well and the
Community delighted in the story of one child and her
mother who arrived at Lee Abbey after dark. When the
little girl woke up the next morning and looked out of
her bedroom window she exclaimed: 'Mummy, is this
heaven?'

An on-going concern for many Community members
was the very middle-class image of the guests and the
difficulty of attracting people from a wider social background. During the eighties, however, it was traditional
Lee Abbey guests, such as doctors, teachers and nurses,
who were having to come to terms with pressures which
they had not previously experienced. Stress was now a
big issue. Houseparty programmes had to take this into
account. Guests wanted teaching and worship, they also
wanted help to relax and be still with God. The popularity
of 'Christ in Quiet' reflected this. It was introduced in the
1970s and consisted of twenty minutes in chapel before
the evening meal, comprising silence and music with very
few words. It could not have been more simple, but it met
a need that was not being addressed in many churches.
It remains a regular feature of the weekly programme,
though often now at the end of the day. Guests continue
to speak of the time of quiet in the chapel as one of
the significant times of blessing during their stay at
Lee Abbey.

As had happened in the seventies the creative arts
again began to take on renewed significance and played
an important part in enabling guests to understand
and experience the love of God. There was a further
move away from the lengthy teaching evening epilogues, that had been at the heart of Lee Abbey's
evangelism in the early days. With increasing use of
drama, music, dance and testimony, most weeks would
include a whole evening's presentation offered by the
Community. Five successive years saw the production
of a major musical based on a biblical theme written
and presented by the Community. These were a full

expression of the creative gifts that so often blossomed from sharing Community life and marked the mutual trust and encouragement that was developing. It was not only the Christmas pantomime that revealed the great sense of fun that lay behind the experience of community! They were a clear demonstration of the transforming power of the Holy Spirit in the lives of the Community, but this also spilled out into the lives of the guests where the creative arts were a catalyst for the on-going healing work of God, for which so many were seeking.

Throughout its history guests have testified of experiencing God's healing whilst staying at Lee Abbey; of head knowledge becoming heart knowledge; of hurts being faced; and burdens relinquished. For many, healing will come from facing the need perhaps to forgive or to accept forgiveness. It may be walking alone in the woods, praying in the quiet atmosphere of the chapel, talking with a Community member or fellow guest, or during the final service of a houseparty or conference that many people have found unexpected healing. Almost every week would include an opportunity for the ministry of prayer with the laying on of hands, whether in a separate service or as part of a final Communion service. It was noticeable that guests who would have been reluctant to come forward for prayer in their local church, would come forward to seek prayer at Lee Abbey. As one guest wrote after a time of ministry 'It is wonderful after so long – as long as I can remember – to be delivered from fear that gripped me to the very depth of my being. I know now what it means to live in the glorious liberty of the children of God.'

The growing demand for quiet and reflection resulted in retreats becoming part of the annual programme. Lee Abbey proved to be a good place in which to introduce people to the experience of retreat, especially for evangelicals, who felt daunted at the prospect of a silent retreat. There was care to help people to draw nearer to God in silence and stillness. Unlike a traditional retreat, silence would be introduced gradually, perhaps from 9.30 p.m. at night until after lunch the following day and then a longer silence later in the retreat. The estate offered sufficient space for those who wished to be alone with God throughout the time. The Lee Abbey programme continues to include at least two retreats each year.

The need to help people find stillness in an increasingly stressful society prompted John Perry to talk with Stan Gorton, the Building and Maintenance Manager, about creating a small chapel, a place for private prayer, somewhere on the estate away from the main house. John's idea had been for a small place somewhere in the woods, but Stan suggested converting one of the old 18th-century lime kilns beneath the chalet on the beach. Here it could be used by guests and visitors alike. Stan took great care clearing out the lime kiln and creating the chapel, constructing the pews himself from wood from the estate. Today the Ley Chapel – Ley means a running stream – provides a place of prayer and tranquillity to countless visitors.

However, Stan was not to know that peace himself, for ten months later he took his own life. His tragic death was a severe blow to the whole Community, but especially to John who had worked closely with him for six years, not least on constructing the Ley Chapel. It was just after the fortieth anniversary of D-Day and Stan and his wife Olive had returned to the Normandy Beaches where he had landed on D-Day. Stan had been one of the first people to enter Belsen at its liberation, and the experience had left a deep scar of inner suffering.

A couple of years before, another death had touched the whole Community. Ursula Kay had joined the Community in 1955. She had run the farm, and the tea cottage, and came to embody the particular ministry of

Lee Abbey for many people. She loved and served God through His creation, and her nature walks at all times of the year opened the eyes of guests and Community to the wonder of God the Creator and Redeemer. She was a woman of prayer, and of great wisdom, though she liked to keep a distance from the politics that is a part of any group of people working and living together. It was with considerable reluctance that she was a member of the Chapter, but her wisdom was invaluable and diffused many potentially tense situations. Like her friend Lil, who had died in 1963, Ursula developed cancer. While her physical body grew weak, she continued to lead life to the full and even within the last weeks of her life was making jars of marmalade. After weeks of unremitting rain and high winds, it was a gloriously sunny day in February 1984 when Ursula died. To all at Lee Abbey in Devon it seemed that the whole of creation was welcoming her to heaven. The nature museum by the road that leads to the beach remains as a testimony to Ursula's unique ministry.

Ursula had provided a vital sense of continuity with the early days of Lee Abbey, and her death marked a further distancing from those early pioneering days. It was not easy for those joining the Community in the eighties, with the atmosphere of prosperity and stability, to sense the spirit of daring faith that had characterised the work forty years before. Edna Madgwick and Audrey Copping were now the only Community members who had joined in the fifties, but they were now retired. They continued as Community members, as the Pelton House, which in the early days when Lee Abbey had generated its own electricity, had housed the Pelton wheel, was converted to form two retirement homes.

This same distancing from the early days was also true for the Council. Those who had been involved in Lee Abbey's founding were now growing old, and within a space of a few years towards the end of the eighties several of the key people who had been used by God in establishing Lee Abbey were to die, including Gordon Strutt, Cuthbert Bardsley and Geoffrey Rogers.

The sense of the end of an era was reinforced in 1987 when Roger de Pemberton, the first Warden, died. Few doubted that without his initial enthusiasm and vision Lee Abbey would never have come into being. Yet when Jack Winslow wrote the first *Lee Abbey Story* in 1956 Roger de Pemberton's name did not appear. He merely wrote of a man 'with a full measure of business acumen and with the temperament which is not afraid to take a risk in a good cause'. Through personal circumstances Roger had left ordained ministry, and it was felt that his name, and so those of the other founders, could not appear in the book. It was not until 1975 when he was invited to take part in the thirtieth anniversary celebrations in the Royal Festival Hall that Lee Abbey was to publicly acknowledge him. However, it was an uneasy reconciliation. Roger de Pemberton's part in the founding of Lee Abbey was not generally known by the Community until the first edition of this book, *Growing in Faith* in 1982. Just a few years before he died John Perry invited him and his family to stay in the house. At Lee Abbey's heart is the story of great faith and great frailty, a reminder that these two often go together. Today his name is remembered in the garden at the centre of the new Community accommodation.

Chapter 13
Faith in the City

Throughout the eighties it was customary to give each new Community member a copy of the book *Life Together* by Dietrich Bonhoeffer. It had been written by the German theologian on the eve of the Second World War, and was the nearest that Lee Abbey has ever come to having a model for its community life.

'Our community with one another consists solely in what Christ has done to both of us. This is true not merely at the beginning as though in the course of time something else were to be added to our community; it remains so for all the future and to all eternity.'

It was a book rooted in reality, 'He who loves his dream of a community more than the Christian community itself becomes a destroyer of the latter, even though his personal intentions may be ever so honest and earnest and sacrificial.'

During the eighties there was to be fresh debate about the significance of community.

On the first evening of every houseparty or conference the welcome to guests would include an explanation that Lee Abbey was the home of a Christian community, but few guests really grasped the significance of that. Many people would sense that Lee Abbey had a special atmosphere, and that it was a place where one encountered the presence of God in a special way, yet few could really recognise the source of that as being the community life that is being lived out, often painfully and falteringly.

While there has never been any attempt to hide the community dimension of Lee Abbey's work, in practice most Community activity such as morning prayers and Community meetings takes place behind the scenes, and it is only rarely that guests will be present at a Community event such as when somebody makes their red label promises.

For most Community members their understanding of community is something that is only grasped slowly, and normally it takes quite a few months at Lee Abbey before Bonhoeffer's book begins to make any sense. Few people will join the Community primarily for the community experience itself: for most people it is an opportunity to share in the ministry. Sometimes it can be observed that those who are most concerned to experience community are those who actually find the experience the most difficult.

Thinking about the significance of community in the eighties was led by John Poulton, a member of the Council, who was to become chairman on the retirement of Bishop Denis Wakeling. John was a humble man, with a great vision for evangelism, eager to find ways of interpreting the Gospel in contemporary society. He was a prophet, in the true meaning of that word, and like all prophets was not always satisfied with the traditional structures. With CMS he had taught theology in Uganda; he had worked for the World Council of Churches, and been Executive Secretary for the Archbishop's Commission on Evangelism. He was excited by the opportunities that he believed Lee Abbey offered for evangelism in Britain. At the Council weekend in 1981, he presented a paper on 'Community as a sign for the future', that was to prove to be truly prophetic in the coming years.

At a time when society in Britain was fragmenting, the Community realised that what they had been discovering, painfully, fitfully and joyfully, about community was something that needed to be rediscovered by the whole Church. The calling of every Christian congregation is to be a community; seeking to be a body of people who express in their disunity, their unity in Christ and their sense of joy, adventure and discovery in life together.

In the advancing spirit of individualism and materialism that was to characterise the eighties, the challenge to form community was the challenge to establish a counter-culture. This was not the call to an easy life. People who believe that community, at Lee Abbey or anywhere else, is easy are quickly disillusioned. The call to community is the call to sacrifice and self-giving – the very opposite to the goals of success and self-fulfilment that were being proferred. New Community members could feel frustrated until they grasped that serving Christ was as much about loading the dishwasher and cleaning lavatories as giving a testimony and praying with those in need. The call to community was not the call to independent self-sufficiency, but the call to give life away. The experience in Lee Abbey was that when Community was seeking to do this, then the Spirit of God could be released for His work.

In seeking to work out the call to community, John Poulton challenged the Council to consider a new expression of community life: a third Lee Abbey which sought to identify with the disadvantaged and to experience community in a tough situation. Without this he believed that Lee Abbey's witness lacked integrity. The inner city was an area in which Lee Abbey in Devon and also in London, realised that they had little experience. Few guests came from such areas, and mission invitations came largely from suburban and more affluent areas. It was realised that brief visits from mission teams would be wholly inadequate, and what was needed was a small Community household that could be part of the ongoing life of the Church and the area.

John Poulton's ideas were reinforced with the publication of *Faith in the City* in 1985, a hard-hitting

report about the state of the inner cities. There was
a great concern that the new venture to establish a
community in the inner city should be a response
to the call of God and not merely an attempt to
counter Devon's 'middle-class' image and appease a
social conscience. John Poulton, the true prophet, was
convinced. 'The new commitment to a Lee Abbey work
elsewhere is more than a whisper from God. It seems
to be "required" it is a question of obedience, out of a
spirit of gratitude.'

A Council working party chaired by Denis Wakeling
clarified the vision. The Community must be residential, living in the area and not coming in from outside
like many other professionals; it must be small, no
more than five or six or it would overwhelm; it must
be long-term, a brief involvement and then to with-
draw would be perceived as merely patronising and
counterproductive; any involvement must be at the
invitation and with the support of the local church.
There was nothing new about the idea of small community households of Christians in disadvantaged areas.
For many years USPG had been setting up Root Groups
with young people serving for a year, and religious
communities like the Franciscans had small houses
in inner cities. It was important that a Lee Abbey
community in the inner city should be part of the
Lee Abbey vision of evangelism through community.
This had been the vision of Bonhoeffer – a community
committed to Christ and to one another, living and
serving others together. It is this which provides a
sign of hope and which creates the atmosphere where
questions can be asked and where people are welcomed
and accepted. Lee Abbey was not going into the inner
city to conduct evangelistic campaigns, neither was it
going in to do amateur social work, where it would
quickly be overwhelmed by the need. The calling was
'to be' not 'to do'; it was essential to live in the place
with no fixed agenda. Such a calling made it very hard

when the new community was first set up, to answer
the inevitable question 'What are you going to do?'.
The answer had to be 'I don't know'.

At the Council weekend in 1986 the formal decision
was made to establish a third Lee Abbey Community.
Although John Poulton played a major part in the
weekend it was clear that he was very ill. He was
not to see his vision realised, for at the beginning
of January he died. However, the vision was eagerly
taken up by John's successor as chairman of the
Council, Simon Barrington-Ward, Bishop of Coventry.
It was in full accord with his own thinking. As General
Secretary of CMS he had written of the call of the
Church to be community, speaking of the Church as
'a fellowship of the unlike, as a sign of the Gospel'.
It was agreed that the West Midlands was to be
the area where the community should be established,
and a second working party was appointed to explore
possibilities in the Birmingham and Lichfield dioceses.
Eventually an invitation was accepted from the parish
of St James' Aston in Birmingham to establish a Lee
Abbey household community.

The parish was predominantly Asian and Muslim,
though the congregation was mostly Afro-Carribean.
It was the area where the Afro-Carribeans first settled
in Birmingham in the fifties and brought up their
children, who then married and moved out to other
suburbs. Many Pakistanis had moved to England in
the seventies, the Bengalis had often been there longer.
Only a short time before, the Lozells Road had become
headline news with pictures of violent street rioting.

Shortly after making the decision to form a community in Aston, a suitable house in the parish, 121
Albert Road, became vacant and Lee Abbey purchased
it. The next task was to draw together community
members. A conference for all those interested in the
new venture was held in Aston in September. As they
sought together to know God's will, some significant

things were said. A black man stated 'I know you think it should be a mixed, black and white, community but I think you will have to put up with starting all-white. We don't understand what you mean by community.' This gave those setting up the community a freedom which only a black person could give, so each person offering for community could be considered irrespective of racial background. In practice the Community has normally been racially mixed, but the freedom was important. There was also a strong sense at the conference that it did need somebody from Lee Abbey, with experience of community to get the new venture started.

As a result of the conference, Dave Rogers felt the call of God to offer for the new community. This underlined that Aston was very much part of the Lee Abbey vision, for his family had been involved with Lee Abbey from its very beginnings; his grandfather, Geoffrey Rogers, being the second Warden in Devon, and his father and mother being involved for many years in leading the Summer Camps. Audrey Martin-Doyle, a chaplain in Devon was asked to be the leader. It was an obvious choice. Audrey had felt a call to work with the disadvantaged for many years. However, she had known nothing of this project when she had joined the Devon Community as chaplain two years before. Immediately she had been attracted by the project and had played a full part in the working party.

Audrey and Dave moved into the house just before Christmas in 1988 and on December 14th in St James' Church Aston, Audrey was licensed and Dave took his full Community promises.

With a lot of help from Lee Abbey Friends and wellwishers work began in turning the house into a home. Three further Community members joined the following year, bringing the total to the maximum of five. However, this was not to be maintained, and the coming and going of Community members has marked

the life of the Aston Community as it does both Devon
and London. Very seldom has the house been full
and at times the Community has been reduced to a
single person. The recruitment of suitable people, with
evangelistic hearts called by God to sacrificial living in
the inner city continues to be a major concern.

From the outset it was decided that Aston should
adopt the same basic community structure as Devon
and London. So there are Community promises which
each member makes on arrival and full Community
promises after the probationary period of three months.
Each member receives a weekly allowance, and any
money received through paid employment is pooled.

Because the first calling of the Community was 'to
be' rather than 'to do', the ministry of each Community member was to develop in a different way as
they became involved in the local community. For
some this would involve paid employment, for others
being involved in local voluntary organisations. One
Community member, Juliet, was a careforce worker
at a neighbouring church; another, Trevor, worked at
the Scripture Union Bookshop in Lozells Road. Dave
became involved in a number of local projects including
the Aston Residents Association, through which he got
to know the president of the local mosque. Another
member worked part-time at the United Evangelical
project legal advice centre, which had been set up
through the vision of a local black Pentecostal minister.
Audrey, as a deacon, was involved in ministry in the
diocese, and spent much of her time seeing people who
came for prayer counselling. It soon became clear that
it was not 'the Community' which would be doing
things but the invidual members called by God. The
house was to be a base from which the members would
go out, undergirded with prayer, either to work or visit
or be involved in something in the area, but it was also
a place to which people would be brought back, a place
of hospitality, counselling and prayer.

Praying together was an essential part of the Community life as in Devon and London. There was the daily morning Community prayers and the weekly corporate Communion service, which with no priest on the Community, was led by different clergy from the Aston area. This in itself encouraged mutual fellowship with the local churches. In addition time would be spent in prayer for the area and for its specific needs.

Hospitality was an important aspect of the life of the Community. Local people were always being invited to the house, but particularly on the first Tuesday evening of each month when there would be a time of worship, prayer and Bible reading followed by a 'bring and share' meal. It was a good time to invite enquirers who wanted to meet the Community and see the house.

The Community quickly realised that they had much to learn from their Muslim neighbours who, at their special festivals, would leave gifts of food on the doorstep of 121. They demonstrated much about commitment to family, caring for elderly relatives and the attitude of being prepared to spend time with people. In seeking to get to know their neighbours, the Community became aware of some of the barriers which had been built up over the years. Most of the Pakistanis in the road had come to England in the seventies, leaving a 'Muslim' country and coming to a 'Christian' country. They assumed that everything allowed in Britain was 'Christian' so all they saw on television, read in the newspapers, watched on videos was presumed to be 'Christian'. It was not surprising that it was considered that Christianity was immoral and something to be despised. It became important that the Community, calling itself Christian, should be a witness to true Christian faith, for they would be watched and evaluated. They certainly were. The shopkeeper and his family living opposite knew all the comings and goings at the house; when the Community had its prayer time in the morning, and even when someone returned from holiday. Dave had spent time helping them when they moved in and was invited round to meals. A white family moved next door to 121 and the wife had been nervous when Audrey went round to welcome them. A few days later she seemed happy to chat, explaining 'the man in the shop said you were all right'! It felt as though the Community had been accepted.

The vision for Lee Abbey Three, as it came to be called, had been for a number of household communities. The experience in Aston encouraged Lee Abbey to establish further household communities in the inner city. So, in April 1991 an invitation was accepted from the Knowle West Ecumenical Steering Group to establish a community on a 1930s housing estate in Bristol. A third household community was established in Walsall in October 1993 at the invitation of the Walsall team ministry.

As the vision, being pioneered in Aston, Bristol and Walsall is worked out, it is hoped that further such communities will be established living under the same basic Lee Abbey rule of life. There would be no difficulty in finding invitations from churches to come to an area, or in obtaining suitable housing. After six years, it is clear that the challenge is to find suitable Community members – Christian men and women who will respond to the call of God to live with the disadvantaged, and be in the front line of the mission of the Lee Abbey movement.

Chapter 14
Space for God

After eleven and a half years as Warden in Devon, John and Gay Perry completed their time at Lee Abbey in 1989 and moved to Hampshire on John's appointment as Bishop of Southampton. At 6.30 a.m. on a cold morning in early January it was still dark as they drove quietly away, having said their farewells at an emotional Community meeting the previous evening. As they approached Top Lodge, where the estate leads into the Valley of Rocks, they saw that each side of the road was lined by the entire Community with torches, singing 'You shall go out with joy'. It was a repeat of that day, twenty-four years before, when Geoffrey and Dora Rogers had completed their time on the Community. Everybody knew that John and Gay's departure marked the end of a significant era in Lee Abbey's history.

The Council appointed as the new Warden, Mike Edson, with his wife Frances. While in 1977 some people might have questioned the wisdom of appointing somebody closely connected with the Renewal Movement, it was now unthinkable that the new Warden would not be identified with charismatic renewal. However, the Renewal Movement had developed greatly in the twelve years since John's appointment. The Council's concern was that the new Warden should build on what John had done, rather than simply continue it. Particularly they sought a man who would develop the spirituality and prayer life of the Community.

Mike came from Nottinghamshire, taking pride in
having been baptised in the church where Robin Hood
married Maid Marian! He had worked in management in industry before training for ordained ministry at Mirfield. For the previous seven and a half
years Mike and Frances had been at St Andrew's
Roxbourne in Harrow and before that in North Devon,
only twenty-one miles away from Lee Abbey at Holy
Trinity, Barnstaple. Here, they had renewed their
contact with Lee Abbey which had first begun at
an Ordinands' Conference in 1972. They both valued
Lee Abbey's ministry, and Frances had been greatly
blessed by God at a Lee Abbey Retreat just before
their move to Harrow. With their Anglo-Catholic background they brought experience of a spectrum of Christian spirituality to the life of the Community.

It was immediately evident to the Community that
Mike's style of leadership was going to be very different. During the first months, he and Frances got
first-hand experience of Community life, by spending time working in the different departmental work
teams. Mike was concerned to develop and deepen the
community dimension of Lee Abbey's work, and this
was to mark the next five years. Some people feared
that the concern for the Community might be at the
expense of the guests.

One of Mike's immediate concerns was to reduce
what he perceived to be the undue stress that marked
Community life, seen in the amount of stress-related
illness among Community members. One cause of this
stress he believed to be spiritual, and he was concerned
to strengthen the individual prayer life of Community
members.

In his first Warden's charge to the Community, he
spoke about personal prayer.

If God is first, then first be with God! . . . for
Christians, this is a statement for action, to state

where our security lies. It is the rock on which we build the rest of our lives . . . being with God is not 'time off work'. It is Sabbath time – being with the Lord so that the Lord is with us in all our time for the rest of the day.

It was the same truth that Bonhoeffer had expressed in *Life Together* when he wrote of 'the Day alone', and had warned, 'Let him who cannot be alone beware of community', and also that Jack Winslow had stressed in his call for the morning watch. It could no longer be assumed that young Christians joining the Community, even from traditional evangelical backgrounds, had established a personal discipline of private prayer at the beginning of each day. Here, Mike sensed, was one source of the stress that the Community was experiencing. He made a change to the daily work pattern by introducing a Community quiet time. Each morning after Community prayers every Community member, other than those directly involved in caring for the guests were to spend half an hour in private prayer. This had always been expected of Community members and was part of the Community promises, but now a specific time in the busy daily timetable was set aside for it.

When, after two years as Warden, Mike wrote a book incorporating much of his teaching to the Community in his first two years, the theme was relationships. He believed that again God was calling the Community to deepen its relationships with one another, and that it was through the quality of its relationships that the Community would witness to the guests, and so to the wider Church and world. In the first chapter of his book – *Loved into Life* – he wrote

The human was not made as an 'individual' but was created in relationship with others and for relationships with others. Life comes through and is experienced within relationships. That is why we are loved into life, because love always demands an 'other someone who is prepared to unconditionally entwine his or her spirit and life with ours.

Mike believed that the Community should reflect this teaching it its life. This was no new theme and was restating in 1990 what Jack Winslow had spelt out forty years before. He had also seen relationships within the Community as crucial to God's work at Lee Abbey. 'No less important than the quality of the inner life is the quality of the outgoing relationships between the committed members of the Community; and here it is that perhaps the most challenging test has to be faced.'

This was to be a continual theme during Mike's time as Warden, but in encouraging the Community to return to the challenge to seek deeper and more open relationships with each other, he was to experience the same frustration that had been expressed by nearly all his predecessors as Warden both in Devon and London. This was the high turnover in Community members. The majority of Community stay for one or two years, and this means that there is at least a fifty per cent changeover in membership each year. An additional problem was that there was now no longer the long-term core of older members that there had been in the past and who had provided stability. In 1990 there were only four, Edna and Audrey who were both retired, and Rodney and Margo Leeson who had been on the Community ten years before. Mike was concerned to build a community that was more balanced in age and maturity. In 1993 he was able to report to Council that there were now seventeen Community members over the age of forty.

Mike also sought to strengthen the Community by

creating a greater sense of consultation and involvement in decision making. The fortnightly Community meetings became far less structured, with more opportunity for every member to contribute. There were also changes to the membership of the Chapter. The weekly Chapter meeting consisting of the Warden, departmental leaders, chaplains and senior Community members had been the main decision-making group within the Community. Mike sought to make Chapter more representative, by bringing in two elected Community members and having one elected chaplain instead of the four. However, now Chapter only met monthly to discuss general policy and there was a feeling that it was at the weekly departmental leaders and pastoral team meetings that most decisions were made.

His concern to encourage greater Community involvement was not so much a concern for democracy, as a belief that God would want to speak through every Community member in directing Lee Abbey's life. This was seen in the drawing up of the vision statement. Mike was concerned to clarify the vision of the Community not just in Devon, but of the whole Lee Abbey movement.

He wanted to encourage people, as he put it, 'to dream dreams and have visions' and undertook a vision-building exercise firstly with the Community, then with the Council at the December weekend in 1990, and then with the Friends at a special midweek conference the following January. Each person was encouraged to wait on God individually, and then to share those experiences, however unlikely they might be, in a small group. A clear consensus emerged from these times of seeking God, and taking all that had been shared, Mike, and a small group of Council members, drafted a vision statement for the whole Lee Abbey movement. The statement did not mark any major change of direction, but rather articulated and clarified the calling of God. A new emphasis

was placed on worship, and so the statement began:
'Lee Abbey believes that it is called by God to be
a worship-based community in which service must
spring from worship so that service becomes worship,
conscious of the beauty of Christ, being loved, being
forgiven, having stillness through silence, receiving the
Holy Spirit, in order to minister'.

The statement also included a renewed emphasis on
the life of Community; rather than now stating that
Lee Abbey existed to serve the Church, Lee Abbey was
to be 'a sign gift for the whole community and to the
world'. 'Lee Abbey exists to embody the Gospel and
models evangelism and discipleship through community, simplicity, commitment, brokenness (repentance),
and sacrifice held in tension with accepting, honouring
and affirming each other, growing into our gifts.'

Lee Abbey in Devon, London and Aston were equally
committed to this vision statement, and each Community worked out the implications for its own life. In
June 1991, Mike put forward a policy document for
Lee Abbey, Devon; the proposals were grouped together
under the headings – the Search for Space. Space
for Training; Space for Worship; Space for Mission;
Space for Friends. They were all rooted in Mike's deep
concern to reduce the pressure on the Community, and
to release Community members for effective ministry.
The dilemma was whether this could be done without
reducing the quality of ministry to guests and in the
next three years, before his move to become Archdeacon of Leicester in 1994 many of these proposals
began to be implemented.

The need to create space for training was probably
the most significant proposal that concerned the Community, and the one that was to prove hardest to
achieve. Mike was concerned to address a gap that had
been evident for many years. Many of those who have
served on the Community have gone on to positions
of leadership and responsibility in the Church. The

Community experience has been a valuable preparation for this, but Lee Abbey was failing to provide any specific training in Christian discipleship and an in-depth understanding of the issues of evangelism and community living. There was just not enough space in the programmes other than the few training days during some closed periods. Also, he was concerned to widen the ministry of Community members so that in their second year they would be undertaking tasks that had normally only been done by the pastoral team, taking on more responsibility for the organisation of houseparties and missions, and learning how to preach and minister in prayer. A significant alteration to the Community's pattern of working would be necessary if the time for this were to be made available. It included reorganising the existing four work departments to create a new 'support' team. Here would be a pool of Community members who would be available to help out in the different departments when members were withdrawn to be involved in houseparty teams, mission teams or trainings and also be responsible for ministry to children and young people. It immediately proved to be very valuable in reducing the sense of strain and stress, and the continual feeling in the departments of always being short-staffed because of other Community commitments.

For one department the reorganisation was to prove very radical and contentious. Mike believed strongly that the estate work needed to be reviewed and that the time had come for Lee Abbey to cease its involvement in market gardening and also that the dairy herd should be sold. It was a proposal that made economic sense, for although the dairy herd generated a profit, it required a lot of Community time which could be used elsewhere. The farm, however, and the cows, had been part of the life of Lee Abbey from the early years, and there was a strong emotional attachment to them. Many Community and guests found it hard to accept that the situation had changed, and that small dairy farms such as Lee Abbey's were no longer really viable. It was with a sense of great sadness that the herd was sold in May 1992, achieving twice the selling price that had been expected. The cows were replaced by sheep, it having been decided to use the farm for commercial lamb production. A variety of breeds were purchased including Jacob's sheep, a herd that had originated in Palestine.

The creation of the support team and the reorganisation of the estate created the space for the first training course to begin in autumn 1992. There were placements in London and Aston looking at community and evangelism, a second unit on mission and a third unit on spirituality which included a retreat with the Franciscans at Compton Durville.

The re-establishment of an annual Community retreat was part of the movement to find space for worship. Sister Carol from the Community of the Holy Name, a regular visitor to Lee Abbey was invited to join the Community to bring an added depth to spiritual teaching and to develop the prayer life of the Community, so filling a gap that had been felt ever since the departure of Jack Winslow over thirty years before. There was a change to the format of Community prayers with the introduction of a greater mixture of liturgy with the free worship, and one Community evening per month was set aside as a time for 'Worship and waiting on God'. For guests, the concern was that the worship that was experienced at Lee Abbey should not just mirror worship in the wider Church, but should in itself be a means of renewing the Church especially by demonstrating the intimate link between authentic worship and mission and service. In addition to different Anglican liturgies guests would experience a wide variety of worship styles including Taizé, Iona and Prayer and Praise.

In seeking to establish space for mission, there was a concern that Lee Abbey continued to receive

almost three times more mission requests than could
be followed up. A further development in Lee Abbey's
mission strategy was proposed in implementing a 'Mission Broking' service whereby a church which has had
a Lee Abbey mission team in turn helps by sending a
team to another church. Two parishes in the Coventry
Diocese were to be the first to be involved in this
when a team from St John's Kenilworth, where Lee
Abbey had conducted a mission in 1992, sent a mission
team to a church at Allersley Park the following year.
Bishop Simon wrote enthusiastically of his experience
of speaking at that mission, seeing how a vision had
been caught.

> I began to see what it could mean if the renewal
> and evangelism which characterised Lee Abbey
> teams could spread like wildfire from one parish
> to another. I had a vision of the possibility of
> parishes throughout the Diocese carrying the fire
> of faith and love from one church to the next
> and spreading the faith and thus the conviction
> and the power to evangelise from congregation
> to congregation. I really do feel this could be a
> breakthrough.

In creating space for Friends, Mike wanted to respond
to the clear request for a greater commitment to
Friends that had been expressed at the Friends' Conference. Lee Abbey's commitment to the local church,
meant that there had always been a reluctance to
create separate Friends' groups. However, it was recognised that in Friends there was the opportunity to
create, within areas, associate Lee Abbey communities
which would work for renewal in their areas, and
be a stimulus to creating community within their
local church. There was an enthusiastic response from
Friends when Mike asked those who might be interested in such groups to write to him. Within a year

visits had been made to twelve potential groups. These visits challenged group members to explore the principles of community life as expressed by the Lee Abbey Movement in the context of their relationships within the group. For several groups this raised the question of adopting group promises along the line of the Community promises. However, close examination of the commitment that would be required meant that many individuals decided they needed longer to consider the implications. In May 1994 a number of members of one group were the first to take group promises. Based on the Community promises in Devon, London and Aston they include an important additional promise. 'I am ready to serve my local church in its mission and evangelism and am ready to help others in the group to a clearer and deeper knowledge of Christ through my work and by my words.'

As the Community sought to work out the implications of the vision statement a new concern arose with a noticeable decline in the number of guests, and for the first time for many years the Community could not automatically assume that the house was going to be full for the summer holiday weeks. Like other Christian holiday and conference centres Lee Abbey began to feel the effects of the recession, though the impact was not to be as severe as that experienced by many of their neighbouring West Country hotels.

The need to attract guests to come to Lee Abbey emphasised the need to improve the quality of guest accommodation. During the eighties much had been done to improve Community facilities, but, other than furnishings, little had been done to guest rooms. In the sixties there had been heated debate within the Community about the decision to carpet the corridors and all that that symbolised. The same issues arose again in determining the standard of accommodation that the Community should offer, along with the desire to keep fees as low as possible. The witness of the Community is compromised if accommodation is perceived by guests as being second best – so often assumed to be a characteristic of 'Christian' places.

A programme of refurbishment was begun in 1994 including the reduction in the number of three bedded rooms and the creation of rooms with en suite facilities, requiring the imaginative adaptation of the Victorian building. A lift has been installed to improve access for the elderly and disabled, for whom the house with its many steps and stairs, has always been difficult.

With the vision statement established and with the Community beginning to work out its implications, Mike and Frances Edson moved to Leicester in August 1994. To take over leadership of the Community in Devon the Council has appointed as Warden, Bob Payne, with his wife Jackie. Bob worked as a physicist with the British Welding Research Association and then taught physics for eight years before ordination. For the last four years he had been vicar of the parish of Charles with St Matthias in Plymouth. In his ministry he has always had a great concern for people to meet intimately with God. In his leadership he is eager that Lee Abbey should continue to enable people to be expectant and open to meet with God, and be a place where congregations become more concerned for the wider world.

When Lee Abbey began in 1946, it was unique in the ministry that it offered. Fifty years later there are many places, both in this country and overseas, offering holidays with Christian ministry. There remains, however, something unique about Lee Abbey; not its setting, though it continues to be a vivid demonstration of the beauty of God's creation; but the life of the Community. While individual members come and go, it is the Community which for fifty years has been seeking to live out their commitment to God and to each other that provides the setting in which God continues to meet with people, to change, to heal and to strengthen their daily life. Sometimes this will be in response to a talk or a time of ministry, but often it is just by being in the place. As some guests have recently written to the Community. 'I must express my thanks to God for leading me to Lee Abbey . . . I feel free at last from so much guilt and anxiety. I can breathe deeply for the first time for years, the pain in my chest has gone . . . relationships feel different . . . I am laughing inside . . . God is so good'. 'Lee Abbey is living proof that the Gospel can flourish without people being pushy. To see and feel what blossomed out of the atmosphere of love, friendliness and sensitivity and freedom was quite overwhelming . . . the Holy Spirit was at work.'

Such is the work of God's grace through community.

Postscript

Autumn 1995 marks the 50th Anniversary of the establishment of Lee Abbey. It is right that the celebrations record and pay tribute to the remarkable work that God has been doing for fifty years, and how a daring venture of faith has been so richly honoured. This book is part of that record. However, it is not possible to assess the full significance of this work of God. Not only have countless individuals come to a living faith in Christ, and made significant steps in their Christian discipleship, but many church congregations and groups of Christians have found new purpose and direction from God, through the ministry of Lee Abbey.

The Golden Jubilee Celebrations do not just mark the purchase of the property in North Devon, but more significantly the establishment of the Lee Abbey Fellowship. In 1995 that Fellowship consists of three very distinct and disparate members – the Holiday and Conference Centre in North Devon, the Lee Abbey International Students' Club in London, and the Lee Abbey Household Communities in deprived areas, normally referred to as Lee Abbey Three. All three have developed directly from the call to evangelism, yet they are not easily perceived as a unity. Most people, including Community members themselves generally identify Lee Abbey with one aspect of the work. It is not easy to evaluate and appreciate the three expressions of evangelism through community to which God has called Lee Abbey. It is essential that people should do so, for it is only in the three together that the true

significance of Lee Abbey for the church in England can
be seen. Here is evangelism through community being
expressed in an international setting in the Students'
Club, in the UPA settings of Lee Abbey Three, and the
holiday ministry in North Devon.

Traditionally the ministry in Devon has dominated,
and it is through Devon that most people encounter
Lee Abbey. Devon is the original work, and remains
the strongest of the three, providing the resources of
finance and manpower that have enabled the others to
be established. Yet there is a fine balance between sup-
porting and dominating, and communication between
the three is of supreme importance. A current concern
of the Lee Abbey Council is to find ways of holding
the Communities together in a way that it is not
happening sufficiently at the moment, so that they
can increasingly value and learn from each other's
ministry and experience, and so be a witness to the
church and our nation.

This book has drawn attention to Lee Abbey's very
real strengths, but I hope that it has been clear that
this has never been easy and many mistakes have been
made. In 1995 each area of the work faces very real
challenges. The Community in Devon are no longer
unique in the ministry that they are offering. There are
many places providing holidays in Christian settings,
and there a wealth of conferences and Christian gatherings offering encouragement to Christians. Devon
has to refine, in ways that have not been needed before,
the particular ministry that God has for it and needs to
take care to promote that.

The Community in London have come through the
traumatic events of the last few years but they continue to face major challenges. A major maintenance
programme will be needed if the building is not to
deteriorate; questions about the nature of the Community and the way that it relates to the students still
need to be worked through, and the type of student,

looking for accommodation in London, continues to change.

The 'Lee Abbey Three' household communities are still in their very early stages, and remain fragile. To be fragile may indeed be an essential part of the calling of a community that would seek to live alongside those who are deprived in our society. Lee Abbey Three needs to continue to develop and work out its mission of 'being' and the concern remains of finding the right people who will commit themselves to this style of community life.

The Golden Jubilee reminds Lee Abbey that its roots lie in the call to evangelism through community. This is also the 50th anniversary of the publication of the report 'Towards the Conversion of England', which expressed so much of the thinking of many Christians at the end of the Second World War. Its analysis of the spiritual life of Britain, and of the widening gulf between the church and the general population is as true in 1995 as it was in 1944. Renewal may have transformed and brought new life and vigour to many congregations in the last fifty years yet the gap between the church and the general public grows wider in our society which, with advancing commercialism and secularism is increasingly becoming fragmented and individualistic. Lee Abbey's initial calling was to evangelism, and to encourage the church to be evangelistic. That need is no less today.

Bishop Simon, the chairman of the Lee Abbey council has summed up the situation in this way.

We have to capture not only the heart but also the mind and imagination of a new generation in a way that was not really recognised in 1944. Above all there is a need for evangelism through an ever richer sense of community, a sense of community that is being groped for in vain in our wider society. There must be places where people

come to learn from each other and listen to each
other and where through their mutual listening
and learning, together with much repenting and
forgiving, the Gospel can be expressed anew.

There are many new possibilities that Lee Abbey could
consider. An obvious area is the development of the
household communities. There is the possibility of
establishing further ministries in this country, and
there are the opportunities that will be presented as
Britain becomes more involved with mainland Europe.
With a sense that God may be calling Lee Abbey to
further expressions of evangelism through community
the Lee Abbey council itself is being reshaped to bring
in new members who can help develop imaginative
thinking. So people are being sought who may bring
expertise in areas such as the business world, the
media, creative arts, science and technology, social
justice and environmental issues in addition to those
who bring experience of church leadership and of
religious communities.

Another issue which will be much more difficult for
the council to face is to question whether God calls Lee
Abbey to bring one part of its work to a conclusion.
At one time this had to be seriously considered for
the work in London. It will arise almost certainly
in the individual household communities that make
up Lee Abbey Three. Could there ever be a time
when this would be asked about the work in Devon?
At the moment it would be hard to imagine it ever
happening, but in 1995 it is clear that the calling
of Lee Abbey is more than to the work of the Devon
Community alone.

In the future Lee Abbey, in all three Communities
and in any others that may be established, will continue to wrestle with issues that have run throughout
this book. God's calling has been to evangelism and
ministry through community, and the experience has

been that it is in the quality of relationships in community life, in Devon, London and Lee Abbey Three where the key to the effectiveness of their witness has lain. There will always be the tension between the emphasis there must be on sustaining the community life in itself, and an emphasis on its wider purpose of serving guests and students. There will continue to be the constant need for fine tuning between 'being' and 'doing'.

Throughout the fifty years there has been the frustration that membership of the Lee Abbey Communities has been short term, not merely for the younger members who stay for one to two years, but even in the leadership itself. In London there have been eight wardens in thirty-one years and even in Devon seven wardens in fifty years. The continual turnover in community membership has ensured vitality, creativity and dynamism but has made continuity difficult, and has frustrated any true corporate growth in community. The experience of all three Communities is that a longer-term commitment would deepen the life and effectiveness of the Community. It would mean that issues of community living, that at present can be avioded as people leave, would have to be faced with the inevitable pain, but also with the healing and growth. All three Communities recognise the nees to build up a larger core of long-term members, as there was in the early days of Lee Abbey in Devon.

In future years there will also be the issue of how Lee Abbey's ministry, and particularly that in Devon, relates to the wider church. The fifty years since 1945 have seen a transformation in the position of evangelicals within the Church of England, from being at the outset a distinct group that was perceived as being on the margin of the church, to being now generally seen as the strongest growing movement at the centre of the church. From the beginning Lee Abbey made no secret of its evangelical convictions, yet believed that their calling was to the whole of the Church of England, and so took care that Community membership should reflect this and that guests from all traditions would wish to come to Lee Abbey. One result of this has been that though relationships with evangelical groups within the church have generally been supportive there has been a reluctance on both sides for too close an identification. This has been less true of Lee Abbey's relationship with the charismatic renewal, which has spanned traditional church groupings, yet also here there has been a deliberate reticence to establish a close identification with any one group. It would be very easy for Lee Abbey to identify exclusively with the evangelical/charismatic approach to evangelism. This would be welcomed by many Community members who generally come from such backgrounds, and by many guests, but it could lead to Lee Abbey forfeiting the unique position that it exercises within the churches of this country and so lose its particular significance.

In the last fifty years Lee Abbey has grown and ministered in a rapidly changing society and a rapidly changing church. There can be little doubt that these changes will not only continue but will accelerate. Lee Abbey will need to change with them but it must be change that is under the direction of God who has so faithfully led the Community for these fifty years. There is a strong conviction that God still has major purposes for the ministry of Lee Abbey and that the Lee Abbey story is far from complete.

'Now to Him who is able to do immeasurably more than all we ask or imagine, according to His power that is at work within us, to Him be glory in the church (in Lee Abbey) and in Christ Jesus throughout all generations, for ever and ever! Amen'

Appendix

Chairmen of the Lee Abbey Council

Roger de Pemberton		1944
Cuthbert Bardsley	– Bishop of Croydon	1946
Geoffrey Rogers		1948
Cuthbert Bardsley	– Bishop of Croydon	1950
	– Bishop of Coventry	
Gordon Strutt	– Bishop of Stockport	1967
Denis Wakeling	– Bishop of Southwell	1977
John Poulton		1984
Simon Barrington-Ward	– Bishop of Coventry	1987

Wardens of Lee Abbey – Devon

Roger de Pemberton	1946
Geoffrey Rogers	1950
Ken Pillar	1965
Geoffrey Paul	1971
John Perry	1977
Mike Edson	1989
Bob Payne	1994

Wardens of the Lee Abbey International Students Club

Gordon Mayo	1964
Chris Hayward	1971
David Johnson	1974
Derek Barnes	1977
John Watson	1981
Mike Battison	1983
David Littlefair	1989
David Weekes	1994

Lee Abbey addresses:

Lee Abbey
Lynton
Noth Devon EX35 6JJ
Tel: 01598 752621
Fax: 01598 752619

The Lee Abbey International
Students' Club
57–67 Lexham Gardens
London W8 6JJ
Tel: 0171 373 7242
Fax: 0171 244 8702

COMMUNITIES

by Jeanne Hinton
Photographs by Christopher Phillips

The stories and spiritualities of twelve European
communities are examined in this inspiring and
informative book. What makes each distinctive? How
does each fulfil its role in society? How does each live
apart from the world - yet in the world? How does
living together really work?

Jeanne Hinton spent several months in each of the
communities featured, listening to the stories of
people living the communal life and seeking discover
the heart of each community and the reasons they
exist, and flourish, a thousand years after the height
of monasticism. Her text, combined with Christopher
Phillip's photographs, give us an insight on to a
moment in the lives of these diverse communities.

The communities featured are:
Lee Abbey (Devon), **Little Gidding** (Bedfordshire),
Bruderhof (Hampshire), **Iona** (Scotland), **Post
Green** (Dorset), **Stepney Franciscan Friary,
Corrymeela** (Ireland) **L'Arche** (France), **Ekklesia**
(Netherlands), **Offensive Chister Jungen**
(Germany), **Grandchamp** (Switzerland) and **St
Eggidio** (Italy).

0 86347 070 X
Eagle

SIMEON AND JOHN

MUSIC TO SOOTH THE MIND AND THE SPIRIT

In 1985, whilst studying at Trinity College of Music, London, Simeon Wood and John Gerighty started out on a journey together which has resulted in a successful partnership as professional performers. In 1989 they joined the community of Lee Abbey where they began to develop an individual style of performance and sound - particularly through their own compositions.

Under the Eagle label Simeon and John have produced four albums:

Reaching Out
(Tape: 0 86347 026 2)
Their first solo album featuring or original compositions interpreted through panpipes (Simeon) and the classical guitar (John).

In the Beginning
(Tape: 0 86347 069 6)
(CD: 086347 082 3)
Quieter melodies composed by Simeon and John, balanced by interpretations of Satie's *Gymnopedie No 1* and Gershwin's *Summertime.*

Impressions
(Tape: 0 86347 099 8)
(CD: 0 86347 100 5)
Featuring arrangements of classical favourites such as Debussy's *Clair de Lune*, Bach's *Sheep May Safely Graze* and Pachelbel's *Canon.*

The Journey
(Tape: 0 86347 120 X)
(CD:) 86347 121 8)
The latest album from Simeon and John marks a broadening of their style and contains 50 minutes of lively compositions on pan pipes, flute and classical guitar, including *El Condor Pasa.*

Practical ways of living in the truth.

1. Keep unmasking the world around us
2. Look for people & places where God's truth
   is spoken
   people who will replenish us – we need
   one another. help people to be real.
3. Listen for God's identity for you.
4. Celebrate your chosenness – every day.
   as a discipline – praise God for
   it – walk in it. — Chosen & Beloved
   Even when "we don't" feel like it
   5 things & which & grateful !

   Implications
   1) makes for real relationship
   2) It takes some & stress out of li

3. lets you free to develop n glow

4. more like Jesus

what does feel when God looks
at you

Zeph 3. 17

MIRE EDSON—

"LOVED INTO LIFE"